PRAISE FOR *RAISING MORE THAN MONEY*

Doug Carter's book is the expression of his own life. It is a coalescing of strength and beauty—strength of character and beauty of compassion. The book blends the force of knowledge with the power of integrity. A must read for all serious stewards.

Rev. Jeff Appling, Senior Pastor
Grove Level Baptist Church, Maysville, Georgia

Doug Carter has hit a home run! Be assured that the principles you'll find for building relationships and raising funds to advance God's Kingdom are presented by a servant leader who has "been there and done that," and better than most ever dream of doing in these vital arenas.

Dave Anderson, President, LearnToLead
Author and Speaker, Agoura Hills, California

Doug Carter is the real deal. His genuine authenticity sets him apart in a crowded field of development professionals. There is a major difference between fund-raising and friend-raising. Doug does the latter with such sincere care that he has become the personification of the vision he is casting. *Raising More Than Money* is exactly that. It's about raising people. After reading this book you will value people in a new way while still resourcing the vision.

Dr. Samuel R. Chand, Samuel R. Chand Ministries Inc.
Author and Speaker, Atlanta, Georgia

If there's one book that I would give a pastor, parachurch leader or non-profit executive on fundraising, this is it! This book could be titled *Fundraising 101*. It is simple but clear, biblical yet practical, relational while being strategic. Doug's life exemplifies everything he writes. If you're looking for a mentor who is doing fundraising right, then Doug Carter's your man! What a gift to the body of Christ!

Rev. Dave Engbrecht, Senior Pastor
Nappanee Missionary Church, Nappanee, Indiana

In *Raising More Than Money*, Doug Carter shares his heart and his passion for the Great Commission and brings clarity to all who find joy in giving. As someone who uniquely knows what it means to serve those who give, Doug offers principles you can embrace and pass on. You will be blessed, and you will be challenged to think about giving generously, joyfully, and strategically.

Karen B. Ford, President, Embrace, Inc.
Author and Speaker, Brentwood, Tennessee

Raising More Than Money communicates the message of Kingdom investing in a way that is both practical and life-giving. But this book is more than just great ideas. You get forty three years of experience of a man who lived it out successfully. Get ready to be blessed!

Rev. Chris Hodges, Senior Pastor
Church of the Highlands, Birmingham, Alabama

Doug Carter has cracked the code in how to raise Kingdom dollars! A long time ago, Doug figured out that the best approach toward raising Kingdom dollars was focus "first" on Kingdom people - their marriages, their children, their needs, their hurts, and their dreams. That was a rather radical approach in some fundraising circles.

Dr. John D. Hull, CEO/President
INJOY Stewardship Services and EQUIP, Atlanta, Georgia

Doug Carter lives the principles in this book. He models generosity and integrity as he helps Christ-followers experience the joy of giving. *Raising More Than Money* is powerful! You must read it.

Dr. Ron McManus, Ministry Consultant and Speaker
Charlotte, North Carolina

I met Doug in 1998 at a John Maxwell conference. I have had the pleasure of developing a strong friendship with him since then. He is a man of integrity, and his passion for the Lord is contagious. His book is a reflection of his love for Christ. This book is vitally important for all Christians who desire to be wise and generous stewards as they give God's resources to Kingdom ministry.

Mike Martin, President, Milton Martin Toyota
Gainesville, Georgia

Doug's life is a picture of a fully-devoted follower of Christ. He is a gift to the Kingdom and so is this book! In it, Doug outlines principles and practices distilled from decades of successful ministry. Read it and apply it, and you'll discover the joy of *Raising More Than Money*!

Mark Miller, Vice President, Training & Development
Chick-fil-A, Inc., Atlanta, Georgia

Doug teaches us how to cultivate a life of stewardship that honors God, inspires others, and impacts future generations.

Dr. Tom Mullins, Senior Pastor, Christ Fellowship
Palm Beach County, Florida

My friend Doug Carter may have written the most important book ever on Biblical giving. From the perceptions of what wealth is and how God wants us to use it, to practical, organized and inspirational advice on how to give, to the step-by-step program for raising more than money, this book covers it all. This is a book to keep on the desk rather than on the bookshelf. There are so many biblical principles laid out that will help keep everyone focused on their specific roles in the body of Christ. This book is destined to be a classic reference and training gem. I found myself saying *Amen* at least twice a chapter.

Larry Plum, President
Cincinnati Casualty Company, Cincinnati, Ohio

Over the years I have learned that a vision without resources to back it up is nothing but a pipe dream. My dear friend Doug Carter has written what I consider one of the most important books that a leader must read. All the leaders I know struggle with raising money for what God has called them to accomplish. Now we have a book that gives us the way to think accurately about raising money and the integrity to do it God's way!"

Rev Dennis Rouse, Senior Pastor
Victory World Church, Norcross, Georgia

Doug Carter is the premier fund raiser in America today. I've learned more about stewardship and donor development from Doug than from any other person. This book will become a standard text for every church leader who wants to develop givers in his or her organization. Without question this book is destined to become a bestseller!

Dr. Stan Toler, Author and Pastor
Oklahoma City, Oklahoma

Doug Carter is living proof of what he says in the book. I have watched him raise up people first. This book has valuable insights for pastors who want to raise up leaders and raise up generous givers in their churches.

Dr. Don Wilson, Senior Pastor
Christ's Church of the Valley, Peoria, Arizona

Raising More Than Money

Raising More Than Money

Redefining Generosity—Reflecting God's Heart

Doug M. Carter

Senior Vice President of EQUIP

with a Foreword by John C. Maxwell

THOMAS NELSON
Since 1798

NASHVILLE   DALLAS   MEXICO CITY   RIO DE JANEIRO   BEIJING

Published in Nashville, Tennessee, by Thomas Nelson, Inc.
Thomas Nelson, Inc., titles may be purchased in bulk for educational, business, fundraising, or sales promotional use. For information, please email SpecialMarkets@ThomasNelson.com.

Scripture quotations marked NIV are taken from the *Holy Bible, New International Version.* Copyright © 1973, 1978, 1984 by International Bible Society. Used by permission of Zondervan Publishing House. All rights reserved.

Scripture quotations marked NKJV are from THE NEW KING JAMES VERSION. Copyright © 1979, 1980, 1982, Thomas Nelson, Inc., Publishers. Used by permission. All rights reserved.

Scripture quotations marked NRSV are from the NEW REVISED STANDARD VERSION of the Bible. Copyright © 1989 by the Division of Christian Education of the National Council of The Churches of Christ in the U.S.A. All rights reserved.

Library of Congress Cataloging-in-Publication Data
Carter, Doug, 1941–
Raising more than money : redefining generosity, reflecting God's
heart / Doug M. Carter ; with a foreword by John C. Maxwell.
p. cm.
ISBN-13: 978-1-4185-1957-5 (alk. paper)
ISBN-10: 1-4185-1957-X (alk. paper)
1. Christian giving. 2. Stewardship, Christian.
3. Generosity—Religious aspects—Christianity. I. Title.
BV772.C375 2007
248'.6—dc22
2007016716

Book design and composition by Mark McGarry, Texas Type & Book Works
Set in Minion

Printed in the United States of America
07 08 09 10 11 — 5 4 3 2 1

Dedicated to biblical stewards
who are investing generously to develop effective leaders
to reach the nations for Christ.

Contents

Foreword   IX

Preface   XI

PART I—STEWARDSHIP:
ACCOMPLISHING GOD'S DREAMS

1   The Heart of the Matter   5
2   Our Response to God's Extravagant Love   17
3   The Link Between Faith and Possessions   23
4   Personal Stories from Today's Christian Stewards   31
5   The Joy of Giving   45

PART II—PARTNERSHIP:
ACCOMPLISHING GOD'S DREAMS TOGETHER

6   The Purpose and Principles of Partnership   53
7   The Power of Partnership   61
8   Pastors and Partnership   71
9   The Pitfalls of Partnership   83

PART III—RELATIONAL FUNDING:
ACCOMPLISHING GOD'S DREAMS THROUGH RELATIONSHIPS

10   Relational Funding: An Overview   97
11   A Closer Look at L.O.V.E. Them   105

12   A Closer Look at L.E.A.D. Them   119
13   A Closer Look at L.I.N.K. Them   129
14   A Closer Look at L.I.F.T. Them   137
15   Keys to Maintaining Strong Relationships   143
16   Life Is About Relationships   149

     Notes   153

Foreword

When Doug asked me to write the foreword for this book, I felt honored. It's been my privilege to call Doug Carter my friend for many years. I first met Doug in 1971, and since that time I have watched him consistently live a life of integrity. The principles Doug shares in this book come from his heart, because he is passionate about sharing biblical stewardship concepts. For Doug, stewardship is first a matter of reflecting God's giving nature; raising money is the by-product.

When God stirred my heart to consider teaching biblical leadership principles in a global setting, I gathered a team who committed themselves to developing effective Christian leaders around the world. EQUIP, a nonprofit global ministry, was birthed, and in 1996 I hired Doug Carter as the first employee. I wanted Doug in my inner circle because of his love for the Lord, his heart for the Great Commission, and his experience as a development officer. Doug not only knows how to raise needed funds, but he truly cares about the donors. He always endeavors to serve them, and he looks for ways to add value to their lives.

From 1997 to 2002, we adapted the leadership materials for an international audience, established relationships, developed partnerships, and listened to key global leaders to understand their unique needs. We also field-tested the resource materials in various parts of the world. In 2002, God placed in my heart a dream to train and resource one million leaders worldwide through EQUIP. What was only a dream in 2002 became a reality in 2006. We are now training over one million leaders on every continent of the world.

The key to EQUIP's success is the principle of multiplication. Every EQUIP-trained leader commits to train at least twenty-five others in his or her community. God willing, we plan to train millions more in the coming years. In this book Doug refers to stories about EQUIP's journey because he has seen firsthand how God blesses biblical relationships, stewardship, and partnerships.

I have often said, "Nothing of significance was ever achieved by an individual acting alone." Doug's vocation in the realm of development has focused more on teaching givers to reflect the giving nature of Christ than about raising money. I'm confident that if you embrace the principles Doug shares in *Raising More Than Money*, it will impact your life for now and throughout eternity. Enjoy the journey.

DR. JOHN C. MAXWELL
FOUNDER OF EQUIP

Preface

This book is for every Christian who desires to give generously, joyfully, and strategically for maximum kingdom impact.

It is for pastors with a God-inspired passion to raise up biblical stewards who experience the joy of investing time, abilities, and financial resources in God's work.

It is for leaders of nonprofit organizations who genuinely believe that their donors are more important than the dollars they give.

It is for "fund-raisers" who believe development work done God's way is not about raising *funds* but about raising *people* to reflect the giving nature of Christ.

L.O.V.E. them.
L.E.A.D. them.
L.I.N.K. them.
L.I.F.T. them.

Thanks to Michael Stephens for his wise counsel that helped to guide me through this book project. It has been a joy to work with him. I am also deeply grateful to my wife, Winnie, and my executive assistant, Karen Hartman, who encouraged me to write this volume and who covered many of my duties so I would have time to write. Also, special appreciation to Anne Alexander, who provided research, editorial assistance, and project consultation. This project would never have been completed without her assistance.

Special thanks to John and Larry Maxwell for inviting me to be the first member of the EQUIP team, and to John Hull, president and CEO of EQUIP, for giving me the freedom every day to practice the principles taught in this book.

Part I

Stewardship:
Accomplishing God's Dreams

Fighting back sleep and struggling to maintain some degree of alertness, I switched the radio from station to station as I drove south on Interstate 75 through central Tennessee. As the clock approached four in the morning, I was losing the battle to stay awake when a radio speaker captured my attention. With great passion in his voice, he exclaimed, "Money is the root of all evil!"

As he continued his diatribe against wealth and all who possess it, he mentioned that he was the pastor of a local church. Immediately I wanted to contact him and point out that he had misquoted the words of the apostle Paul in 1 Timothy 6:10. I also desperately wanted to clear up this young man's misconception. Paul did not say that *money* was the root of all evil; he said the *love of* money was the root of all evil. To remove those two small words from the text changes the whole message.

But this minister's intense disdain for people of affluence came through loud and clear. His attacks on those who had, in his words, "done well" concluded with the following summation: "Money is the root of evil, so the more money a person has, the more evil he is!"

This country preacher is not alone in his near hatred for people who have succeeded in acquiring capital. Many modern politicians often try to pit the "haves" against the "have-nots," because "class warfare" is a key political strategy that candidates can use as a wedge issue.

Many seem to hold the opinion that "doing well" (possessing and accumulating wealth) is the enemy of "doing good" (serving others and making a positive difference). But what about God's great dream of building a kingdom *filled* with the people He loves? To accomplish that, millions of people all over the world who have never heard the gospel will have to be reached. Missionaries will need to be sent. Native-language Bibles and other materials will have to be printed. And that's only the slightest beginning.

So who is going to fund all of that? Big business? Big Brother? Not hardly.

Before we dive into the depths of raising money—and more—let's get personal. The Bible says that Jesus "went about doing good" (Acts 10:38 NKJV). You and I are called to do the same. But with all the "good" that needs to be done in order to achieve God's dreams, an important question surfaces: *Is it possible to do both* good *and* well?

1

The Heart of the Matter

For the love of money is a root of all kinds of evil, for which some have strayed from the faith in their greediness, and pierced themselves through with many sorrows.

—1 Timothy 6:10 NKJV

THE POWER OF MONEY

The Bible has more to say about money and possessions than almost any other subject—more than *two thousand* verses, as compared to five hundred on prayer, and even fewer on faith. Jesus talked about money consistently. Sixteen of His thirty-eight parables deal with it. Why? He understood its power on the human heart. And, indeed, money consumes our waking thoughts and even shows up in our dreams. But *how* we think about it, Jesus said, reveals where our hearts really are.

And where *are* our hearts? People today, from all walks of life, have traded the glory of God's presence for *personal pleasure*. Our culture has gone wild in its quest for it. It is no wonder, then, that multitudes *worship* the one thing they can easily barter for even *more* pleasure: money. That's where the heart of man is these days.

But Jesus said, "You cannot serve God and wealth" (Matt. 6:24 NRSV). Why would He say *that*? Because wealth, or money, has a god-like power—small *g*, but godlike nonetheless,[1] for several reasons:

1. *People love it.* In fact, many give their lives to accumulating more and more of it. But Matthew 22:37 says, "You shall love *the LORD your God* with all your heart, with all your soul, and with all your mind" (NKJV, emphasis added).

2. *It gives us power beyond our immediate circle of influence.* But Jesus promised, "You shall receive power when *the Holy Spirit* has come upon you" (Acts 1:8 NKJV, emphasis added). The indwelling Spirit of God is to be our *real* power source.

3. *It seems to provide us with the things we most desire.* Yet God Himself wants to be our Provider. He alone is Jehovah-Jireh ("the Lord Will Provide"). The Word of God says, "God shall supply all your need" (Phil. 4:19 NKJV). And if that's not enough, the Psalmist proclaimed, "No good thing will He withhold from those who walk uprightly" (Ps. 84:11 NKJV).

4. *The more money we have, the more we want.* This is the attitude we *should* have about the Lord. King David wrote, "My soul thirsts for You; my flesh longs for You" (Ps. 63:1 NKJV),

---

"Money never made a man happy yet, nor will it. There is nothing in its nature to produce happiness. The more a man has, the more he wants. Instead of its filling a vacuum, it makes one."

—BEN FRANKLIN

---

and again, "As the deer pants for the water brooks, so pants my soul for You, O God" (Ps. 42:1 NKJV).

5. *It challenges the true and living God for "first place" in our lives.* But our God insists that *He* reign in our hearts. With His own finger He wrote, on a tablet of stone, "You shall have *no* other gods before Me" (Ex. 20:3 NKJV, emphasis

added). Jesus confirmed this in Luke 4:8: "It is written: 'You shall worship the LORD your God, and Him only you shall serve'" (NKJV).

6. *It can buy pleasure.* But what a cheap—and temporary—substitute for the glory of God in our lives! David sang, "In Your

---

Money is an instrument that can buy you everything but happiness and pay your fare to everywhere but Heaven.

—WAYNE MYERS

---

presence is fullness of joy; at Your right hand are pleasures forevermore" (Ps. 16:11 NKJV). God *alone* brings pleasure that is eternal.

7. *It confronts us with crucial choices that cannot be ignored.* So does God. In fact, He requires us to make the most important choice of all: what we will do with Jesus. "He who believes in Him is not condemned," says John 3:18, "but he who does not believe is condemned already, because he has not believed in the name of the only begotten Son of God" (NKJV). The book of Joshua puts it bluntly and succinctly: "Choose . . . this day whom you will serve (24:15 NKJV).

8. *It has the potential to control our lives.* And if money is our master, then God isn't. Listen to what Jesus said: "No one can serve *two masters*; for either he will hate the one and love the other, or else he will be loyal to the one and despise the other. You cannot serve God *and* mammon [money]" (Matt. 6:24 NKJV, emphasis added). God is adamant that His Son be the Master over all. Saint Paul wrote, "God . . . has highly exalted Him and given Him the name which is above every name, that at the name of Jesus every knee should bow, of

those in heaven, and of those on earth, and of those under the earth, and that every tongue should confess that Jesus Christ is Lord" (Phil. 2:9–11 NKJV).

THE LOVE OF MONEY

Despite money's godlike power, money itself is not evil. It's true that it can be a tool of destruction, but it can also be an agent of healing. By itself, money has no inherent qualities of good or evil. But "the *love* of money," said Paul the apostle, "is a root of *all kinds* of evil" (1 Tim. 6:10 NKJV, emphasis added).

Once, when asked what was the first and greatest commandment, Jesus answered, "Love the LORD your God with all your heart, with all your soul, with all your mind, and with all your strength" (Mark 12:30 NKJV). He leaves no room for doubt: *God* must be the all-consuming love of our lives. But money has the potential of dethroning God as the chief love of our lives. It becomes His rival. The danger is clear.

My dad often stated, "We can worship money and use God, or we can worship God and use money." He understood the heart of the matter: Wealth is neither good nor evil. The role it plays in our lives and how we use it are the big issues.

What role does wealth play in *your* life? Put another way, where is your *treasure*?

WHERE YOUR TREASURE IS . . .

It is impossible to talk about loving God without talking about our hearts. You may have heard it said, "The heart of the problem is the problem of the heart." What did Jesus have to say about the heart? "Where your treasure is," He stated, "there your heart will be also" (Matt. 6:21 NIV). In other words, the desires of our hearts will follow whatever we *treasure*.

Each time we make a purchase, decide on an investment, or give a donation, we communicate what we treasure—what we truly care about. "Checkbooks and receipts reveal our most tightly held values. Whether or not we talk openly about what is most important to us, how we use money gives us away."[2] Our use of money reveals our hearts.

Earlier we discussed Jesus' definition of the "first," or greatest, commandment: *Love God with all your heart, soul, mind, and strength.* But

---

Checkbooks and receipts reveal our most tightly held values. Whether or not we talk openly about what is most important to us, how we use money gives us away.

—PAUL J. MEYER

---

then He went on to say, "And the second [greatest commandment] . . . is this: 'You shall love your neighbor as yourself.' There is no other commandment greater than these" (Mark 12:31 NKJV). As if that wasn't enough, though, Jesus later added, "A new commandment I give to you, that you love one another; as I have loved you, . . . love one another" (John 13:34 NKJV). That changes things considerably!

Jesus' command to love "as I have loved" is thought provoking, to say the least! I think we would all agree that loving others to the extent that He loves us is impossible. Just think about how much He has loved us. As I watched the movie *The Passion of the Christ*, I was forcefully reminded of the price Christ paid for my salvation—and yours. He willingly laid down His life for us who are so unworthy. The prophet Isaiah declared, "He was wounded for *our* transgressions, He was bruised for *our* iniquities; the chastisement for *our* peace was upon Him, and by His stripes we are healed" (53:5 NKJV, emphasis added).

Oh, what a Savior! When we come to Christ in genuine repentance for our sins, bringing all *our* guilt and shame, He abundantly pardons and freely gives us *His* love—and salvation. What an exchange!

    For despair, He gives hope;
        for death, life;
            for defeat, victory;
                for guilt, pardon;
                    for sin, righteousness;
                        for storms, peace;
                          for sorrow, joy;
                            for poverty, blessings;
                              for fear, courage;
                                for brokenness, wholeness;
                          for darkness, light.

The old camp meeting song "Such Love" enthusiastically celebrates God's wondrous affection for us:

    That God should love a sinner such as I,
    Should yearn to change my sorrow into bliss,
    Nor rest till He had planned to bring me nigh,
    How wonderful is love like this![3]

So how can we *ever* love others as God has loved us? We can't, not on our own—we need God. Without His love in our hearts, there is no way we can love others wholly, purely, or adequately. But when we receive Christ, His love is "poured out in our hearts by the Holy Spirit" (Rom. 5:5 NKJV), and when that happens, we want to "pay it forward." We *want* to love as He loved us.

"So, how do I do it?" you say. "And what's that got to do with my money?" I'm so glad you asked.

First, let's look at another very pointed directive from our Savior. In John 14:15, Jesus said, "If you love Me, keep My commandments" (NKJV). That sounds simple enough . . . *until* He reveals to us that overarching mandate, known as the Great Commission, to "make disciples of all the nations" (Matt. 28:19 NKJV). How on earth can we do *that*?

Are you financially blessed? Do you have, not only enough to pay your bills and meet your basic needs, but *more* than enough? *Hmm* . . . Why would God give any of us "extra" of anything—more time, talent, or treasure than we need? Could the key reason be so that we can participate personally in fulfilling the Great Commission? That assignment from God was a direct overflow from His heart of love for a lost world. If this same love is then "poured out in [*my*] heart" (Rom. 5:5 NKJV), shouldn't it move me toward an active involvement in the Great Commission? It should. Any Christian with a heart full of God's love will surely share His concern for the poor and His priority to reach every person on our planet with the good news. But that requires giving money. And that takes us back to our discussion of what we *treasure*.

Jesus said, "Do not lay up for yourselves treasures on earth, where moth and rust destroy and where thieves break in and steal; lay up for yourselves treasures in heaven . . . For where your treasure is, there your heart will be also" (Matt. 6:19–21 NKJV). Practically speaking, then, if we treasure the things of this earth, then *spending* and *hoarding* our money will be the focus of our hearts. But if we treasure the eternal things of God, then we will harness the power of our money as an expression of our love for Him, and our hearts' focus will be *giving*, laying up treasures in heaven.

But what does "laying up treasures in heaven" *look* like, where money is concerned? It begins with the tithe.

BIBLE BASICS OF GIVING

Many today argue that tithing is no longer required of God's people, contending that we no longer live under Old Testament *law*, but under New Testament *grace*. Yet I find it interesting that the giving of a tenth (or "tithe") to God was practiced by Abraham and others long before the Law was given to Moses (Gen. 14:19–21; 28:20–22; Heb. 7:1, 4). I can find no place in the New Testament where the principle of the tithe has been rescinded. And while I believe that God expects New Testament Christians to give both tithes *and* offerings (gifts above and beyond 10 percent), the tithe itself is clearly the *foundation* for biblical giving. In fact, it is dangerous, in my opinion, to refuse to tithe. In Malachi 3, God Himself said that those who fail to tithe are robbers and live

---

"I can't afford to tithe!" you say?
Oh no, my friend. You cannot afford not to.

---

under a curse: "Will a man rob God?" He asked. "Yet you have robbed Me! But you say, 'In what way have we robbed You?' In tithes and offerings. You are cursed with a curse" (vv. 8–9 NKJV). I cannot begin to imagine a more risky way to live than to regularly steal from God. He goes on to say, "Bring all the tithes into the storehouse, that there may be food in My house" (v. 10a NKJV). He is very serious about this command to give Him 10 percent of our income. And look at what He promises to those who do: "Try Me now in this . . . if I will not open the windows of heaven and pour out for you such blessing that there will not be room enough to receive it" (v. 10b NKJV).

Wayne Myers, veteran missionary to Mexico, shares the story of Chanito, a Mexican pastor who was convinced that he was too poor to tithe. One night, after Wayne preached on tithing to a large conference of pastors in Mexico, he, Chanito, and eight other pastors packed into an old car and began a long journey on a narrow, winding road in a mountainous region infested with thieves and robbers. Here is how Wayne tells the story:

I had spoken on the subject of giving in the convention that night, and our conversation just naturally turned to the subject of finances and giving. Chanito confided that he never seemed to have enough money. I immediately knew the root of his problem.

"You don't tithe, do you, Chanito?" I asked him.

"Brother Wayne, I don't have enough money to tithe."

I jerked the car over to the side of the road and came to a complete stop.

"Get out of God's car," I commanded.

We were in a blanket of dark night, miles from the nearest town, and completely vulnerable to whatever and whoever might be lurking in the darkness.

"Why?" Chanito's voice was incredulous.

"Because I am harboring a thief and you are endangering my life."

"You are not going to leave me with the thieves, Brother Wayne," he implored.

"Let the thieves beware of you!" I told him. "I am more afraid of you than I am of them. They only rob men. You have the audacity to rob God."

"Brother Wayne, I promise I will start tithing."

"All right, get in," I conceded. Of course, I would not have left him for a minute on that road. But he got the point.

Chanito began to tithe, and in the end money was only a small part of what he gave to God. He is in Heaven now, but before he died he established congregations in the most difficult parts of Mexico where life is worth very little.[4]

When the offering plate passes in front of a person who has God's tithe in his pocket and keeps it there, indeed, a form of theft occurs. I am amazed at those who say they love God yet ignore this very basic discipline of faith. No Christian can ever learn to practice true biblical stewardship until he first learns to faithfully tithe. Tithing obediently and steadfastly lays the foundation for discovering the privilege of giving *more* than the tithe.

Like our Savior, we are to *grow* in the Lord (see Luke 2:40). In fact,

Peter admonishes us to "grow in the grace and knowledge of our Lord and Savior Jesus Christ (2 Pet. 3:18 NKJV). Sadly, I have met scores of Christians who seem to have grown in every area *except* giving. It is my firm conviction that if one has followed Christ for several years and is still giving only 10 percent, he or she has a lot of growing to do in the realm of stewardship. We *begin* with the tithe; *then* we learn to give "extra"—offerings above and beyond 10 percent. We discover that when we give generously, God gives even more generously. Jesus promised, "Give, and it will be given to you: good measure, pressed down, shaken together, and running over . . . For with the same measure that you use, it will be measured back to you" (Luke 6:38 NKJV).

"But what if I don't have a lot extra?" you may be asking. "What if I barely get by? Shouldn't I wait until I make more money before I concern myself with giving to kingdom work?" Or, if you are trying to raise funds, "Those folks live from paycheck to paycheck. Shouldn't they get their heads above water before I ask them for money?"

In his book *Today Matters*, John C. Maxwell, the founder of EQUIP, states, "People give not from the top of their purses, but from the bottom of their hearts. If you desire to become a more generous giver, don't wait for your income to change. Change your heart. Do that and you become a giver regardless of your income or circumstances."[5] Again, it's a matter of the heart—and a matter of trust.

CHECKS AND BALANCES

God delights in prompting hearts to give for His projects and His glory. When God prompts your heart, you can trust Him with the outcome. But make sure when you give that it is God, and not just your emotions, that is leading you. Giving based on emotions alone can result in bad stewardship of God's resources. There's a balance between keeping your heart engaged and using wisdom in your giving.

Here are some "checks and balances" for heart-prompted giving:

1. Make sure it is the Lord driving your decision to give.
2. Discuss your decision with your spouse or another trusted friend for confirmation.
3. Assess whether or not your giving follows your passions. God tends to call people to support causes about which they are *passionate*.
4. Ask yourself, "Does this project advance God's kingdom?"
5. Make sure you trust and respect the person who is leading the project to which you want to give.

In summary, get to the heart of the matter. Ask yourself, "What do I treasure?" Then give. Just give. Give to fulfill the Great Commission. Give because you love God. Give because you love others. And give because God loves you.

2

Our Response to God's Extravagant Love

Were the whole realm of nature mine,
That were a present far too small.
Love so amazing, so divine,
Demands my soul, my life, my all![1]

—Isaac Watts, "When I Survey the Wondrous Cross"

PIPELINE GIVING

Because God's amazing grace lovingly reached down to meet us in our needy and broken condition, we should respond by loving Him. One way to beautifully express our love for God is by supporting efforts to share His extravagant love with people in need. "I want you to affirm constantly," Paul wrote to a fellow laborer, "that those who have believed in God should be careful to maintain good works. These things are good and profitable to men" (Titus 3:8 NKJV).

In his book *The Cycle of Victorious Giving*, Stan Toler writes about "grudge giving" (feeling forced to give) and "obligatory giving" (feeling obligated to give). "But there is a whole other world of giving," he adds, "a giving that feels good, that warms the heart as it relieves the burden of another, a giving that wells up inside like a spiritual fountain, refreshing the soul, encouraging the spirit, and strengthening the faith. It is grace giving."[2]

Stan also shares in his book some comments from Dr. Tom Phillippe, a member of the board of directors of EQUIP. Tom and his wife, Joan, are known for their generous giving. Tom says, "I learned that I was not to be a reservoir or a bucket. I was to be a pipeline. God would pour His blessings into my life as long as I was willing to pour them out to a lost world."[3]

"Pipeline giving" is delightful giving—sowing out of a heart of gratitude for God's faithfulness. The pipeline giver loves to give because God lovingly gave. But none of us instantly becomes a pipeline giver. For most Christians the journey from "babe in Christ" to mature Christian steward is a rather slow process. But every follower of Christ urgently needs to take this journey. It is the pathway to a grown-up faith and a daily walk with Christ that honors Him and exalts His name in every arena of life. This pipeline-giving journey can be summarized in three stages:

1. The Sons-and-Daughters Stage

When we first receive forgiveness for our sins and are adopted into God's family, we often exhibit the characteristics of babies: we tend to

---

"When God blesses us, He always has more than us in mind."

—RON JUTZE

---

think first of *our*selves and *our* needs. Only as we grow in grace do we begin to understand that we have been "blessed to be a blessing." As my friend Ron Jutze says, "When God blesses us, He always has more than us in mind." As we feed on His Word, we begin to understand that we are called to serve others, and we move to the next stage:

2. The Servant Stage

As we begin to saturate our minds with the Word of God, we discover our call to servanthood; that is, we encounter the proverbial "towel and basin" (see John 13:3–17). With Jesus as our example on the pathway of obedience, we begin to make investments in the lives of others and transition to:

3. The Steward Stage

As we continue down the road, in the middle of the path stands the cross. As we come face-to-face with the cross of Christ, it calls us to bend our wills to conform to His will. It demands a full surrender of our lives to Him. It beckons us to renounce self-centeredness, self-promotion, and self-reliance. And we respond as our Lord did in the Garden: "Not as I will, but as You will" (Matt. 26:39 NKJV). We give up control of our lives, invite Him to the throne of our hearts, and ask Him to rule in our lives in all of His lordship. He becomes Lord of all in every area! We discover that "[we] are not [our] own" and acknowledge that we were "bought at a price" (1 Cor. 6:19–20 NKJV).

WE OWN NOTHING!

As we obediently walk the road of genuine discipleship, it is not long until our hearts and minds come to the realization that *God is the owner of everything*. We own nothing! We are but managers, or caretakers, of what He has placed in our hands. The awesome responsibility of stewardship grips us. Then the wonderful privilege of partnership with God in His rescue plan for a lost world energizes us, and we begin to ask some questions of eternal importance:

1. How much should I give?
2. To whom should I give?
3. How much should I keep?

More than two hundred years ago, clergyman John Wesley, the great revivalist of England, began his ministry earning 30 pounds annually. He made a decision then to live on 28 pounds and give 2 pounds to the local church. Later, when he made 60 pounds, he still lived on 28 but now gave 32 pounds to the church. Eventually, he earned 120 pounds but *continued* to live on 28. He was consistently giving 92 pounds to the local church. His book royalties alone could have made him a very wealthy man, but he chose to give away nearly everything he earned. He recognized that he owned nothing—it was all God's—and thus became a model of Christian stewardship.

John Wesley stated these three financial rules in the printed text for his sermon "The Use of Money":

I.   We ought to gain all we can gain but this it is certain we ought not to do; we ought not to gain money at the expense of life, or at the expense of our health.

II. Do not throw the precious talent into the sea.

III. Having, first, gained all you can, and, secondly saved all you can, then "give all you can."[4]

Throughout his life, Wesley maintained a simple lifestyle. It is not my intention to try to define a "simple lifestyle." This is a matter between God and each of His servants. My intention is to emphasize the need to become, like Wesley, a biblical steward. But it won't happen overnight; it's a process. We must *daily* seek the Holy Spirit's guidance as we endeavor to faithfully practice biblical stewardship, ever mindful of the needs of a lost world and the urgency of reaching the nations for Christ.

Alan Bracken, a successful young business leader in northeastern Tennessee, occasionally seeks my advice on stewardship and an "appropriate" lifestyle. How much of his income should he invest in the expansion of his business? he wants to know. And how much should he place in retirement funds?

He said to me in a recent phone call, "Life is a series of decisions about how I will use the money and resources that God has entrusted to me, never forgetting that He is the owner, I am the steward." He added, "After much prayer and counsel, I recently decided to start a second business for one purpose only: to increase my giving to Great Commission work. Our annual giving goal continues to grow." Alan and his wife, Amanda, are determined that "kingdom investments" will be the largest item on their financial statements. Why? Because they understand the link between their *possessions* and their *faith*.

Do you?

3

The Link Between Faith and Possessions

Take heed and beware of covetousness, for one's life does not consist in
the abundance of the things he possesses.

—Jesus Christ (Luke 12:15 NKJV)

I have spent most of my life in the ministry of development. What a
blessing that has been. And I don't even mind the jokes about fund-
raisers, even when they are aimed at me—like this one:

A very wealthy man and his wife, the sole survivors of a cruise ship
disaster on the high seas, make it to a tiny island in the middle of the
Pacific. There is nothing there but sand and a single palm tree. While
the wife is wringing her hands and wailing in despair, her husband is
very serene.

"How can you be so calm in this terrible situation?" she cries, irri-
tated by his peaceful demeanor. "We will never be found. We will die
here!"

"Don't worry," he replies. "I pledged $100,000 to EQUIP this year.
Doug Carter will find us in no time."

Right you are, mate, because Jesus' words in Luke 12 are absolutely
true: "To whom much has been committed, of him they will ask *the
more*" (v. 48 NKJV, emphasis mine).

Are you blessed materially? Are you one of those to whom "much has been committed"? Then get ready, because Jesus also said, in the same verse, "To whom much is given, from him much will be required" (NKJV). Uh-oh. Sounds like it's time to grow your generosity —and measure your faith.

"The greatest blessings bring with them the greatest responsibilities."

—GEORGE HESTER, CHAIRMAN AND CEO OF NAVITAS,

A VALUES-DRIVEN WEALTH ADVISOR[1]

GROWING YOUR GENEROSITY

"Our use of possessions is an accurate barometer of our faith," says author Wesley Willmer. In his outstanding book *God and Your Stuff,* Wes clearly shows that there is a correlation between soul maturity and the use of assets—a link, if you will, between our *faith* and our *possessions.* A growing faith is ultimately expressed by a growing generosity in our giving.

The journey toward mature faith and stewardship, he says, consists of six stages:

1. *Imitator*: Mimics others' stewardship.
2. *Modeler*: Gives sporadically when there is an example to follow.
3. *Conformer*: Gives because of recognition, tax benefits, and/or other personal gain.
4. *Individual*: Gives in proportion to what God has given him or her.
5. *Generous Giver*: Recognizes that all one possesses is from God, and derives joy from giving.
6. *Mature Steward*: Focuses on God and then on others. The mature steward is more concerned with treasures in heaven than on earth and is content with daily provisions.[2]

I encourage you to locate a copy of Dr. Willmer's excellent book. In it, he offers ten biblical directives for a faithful steward, summarized here:

1. Declare who is Lord of your life.
2. Understand what a faithful steward is.
3. Count your blessings—you have more than you realize.
4. Give to God *first*.
5. Give to God systematically.

"If you want to know what a man is really like, take notice of how he acts when he loses money."

— SIMONE WEIL

---

6. Give according to your means.
7. Give cheerfully.
8. Give regularly.
9. Give to God generously but quietly.
10. Give regardless of your circumstances.[3]

"Why should I do all of that?" you may say. Because it's all God's anyway!

IT'S ALL GOD'S ANYWAY

Many people today are experiencing the joy of mature Christian stewardship. And wherever stewardship is consistently modeled, it is because godly stewards see everything that they possess—be it little or much—as God-given. Their possessions do not "possess" *them*.

"There's nothing intrinsically wrong with having a nice car, living in a comfortable home, or dressing in the latest fashion," says author

Stan Toler, "unless those possessions possess us, unless the pursuit of those things keeps us from pursuing a deeper relationship with the Lord. That's the real danger." He continues:

> Materialism is an enemy of faith. It replaces eternal values with valuables in one's heart allegiance—it considers the temporal (the temporary) more important than the eternal.
>
> People in Bible times were expected to express their commitment to God by what they gave rather than what they gained. It was to be a mark of their spiritual maturity. The standard has not changed . . . At the very core of our Christian faith is the acknowledgment that all material blessings are given by God—they come to us from the storehouse of His love and compassion. He is the source. Our giving is simply the supply line that channels the blessings He has already put in reserve for us. Great missionary statesman, David Livingstone, wrote, "I will place no value on anything I may possess except in relation to the kingdom of Christ. I will use my possessions to promote the glory of Him whom I owe all."[4]

It seems that Livingstone, too, realized that everything he had was God's.

GIVING VERSUS SPENDING

In his powerfully challenging book *The Law of Rewards*, Randy Alcorn argues that giving is the alternative to spending or hoarding. It breaks the back of materialism. "Giving is a joyful surrender to a greater person and a greater agenda," he states. "It affirms Christ's lordship. Giving dethrones me and exalts Him. It breaks the chains of mammon that would enslave me. It makes heaven, not earth, the center of gravity."[5]

My dear friend Dave Anderson, president of Learn to Lead, challenges us with his comments about giving and spending.

Strangely, attaining position and possessions often creates a let-down. It's like the child who, after all the hype and anticipation, opens his final present on Christmas morning and is stricken with the sinking feeling, "Is this all there is?" And while multitudes become successful financially, few live significant lives. In fact,

---

"Contrary to what Hollywood promotes, it is not what you get or accumulate that makes you significant but what you give away; what you contribute, the value you add to others and what you become in the process."

—DAVE ANDERSON

---

when most people reflect upon their years on earth they will realize they did not live a significant life precisely because it was so easy to settle for a successful one. Sadly, when most people die, it will be as though they never lived. Frankly, this is inexcusable because significance is within the grasp of everyone willing to embrace the right priorities. Contrary to what Hollywood promotes, it is not what you get or accumulate that makes you significant but what you give away; what you contribute, the value you add to others and what you become in the process.[6]

So true—yet so *hard* to put into practice.

Over the years, I have had the privilege of building lasting friendships with hundreds of God's people in America and around the world. And, admittedly, those with the most wealth sometimes face a real battle as they endeavor to keep "first things first" and to maintain a lifestyle that faithfully reflects the giving nature of Christ. Frankly, I think *most* of us struggle as we travel this road. There seem to be so many obstacles in our way. Things like:

- resistance—a lack of surrender
- self-centeredness—a lack of humility
- fear—a lack of trust
- doubt—a lack of faith
- indifference—a lack of obedience
- excuses—a lack of commitment
- complacency—a lack of vision
- apathy—a lack of passion
- procrastination—a lack of urgency
- inconsistency—a lack of focus or discipline
- confusion—a lack of information

Recognize any of these roadblocks in your life? Believe it or not, we *can* overcome them, every one. But to do so, we must:

- surrender our lives totally to Christ
- see a lost world through His eyes
- diligently study and faithfully obey His Word
- seek the Holy Spirit's guidance in every decision we make
- stay focused on Christ
- act on His mandate to make disciples of all nations

If you are already doing these things, it could be that you have the "gift of giving."

THE "GIFT OF GIVING"

In his book *The Blessed Life,* Pastor Robert Morris shares the following observations about individuals who give generously—folks who have the "gift of giving":

1. They respond to strong vision with clear objectives.
2. They don't want to be a Band-Aid—they want to be a cure (i.e., bring lasting solutions to a problem).

3. They want to give more than just money—they also want to give their time, their talents, and their wisdom.

4. They are often gifted leaders. In fact, their leadership ability is precisely *why* they have resources to give.

5. They don't appreciate being criticized for their successful lifestyle.

6. They don't want to talk about money all the time. They instead like to talk about their families and what God is teaching them on life's journey.

7. Their discernment allows them to determine genuine needs.

8. They are both very frugal and very generous.

9. They desire to be appreciated but not recognized.

10. They want to invest in a stable ship, not a sinking ship.[7]

FOLLOWING JESUS WITH WEALTH

Recently I came across a powerful testimony by Ed Owens, founder of Samaritan Asset Management Services in Chicago, on the Generous Giving Web site. After sharing the story of his conversion and his journey toward becoming a generous giver, he discusses the biblical account of the poor widow who gave all. Ed states:

> Jesus commends this woman, not for giving away so much, but for keeping so little. When I read this, I want Jesus to call her foolish. Instead, he holds her up as an example for giving away all that she had. My gifts given from wealth are not as valuable to Jesus as I tend to think. In Jesus' view, the amount we keep indicates more than the amount we give . . . Many people saw my generosity and thought I was a good steward. But even in the midst of my giving, I was still keeping a lot for my own personal pleasure. I was mainly giving out of my great wealth, just as the Pharisees had done.[8]

Ed concludes his testimony with a discussion of his efforts to move to a moderate lifestyle with a focus on how much to keep, not the size of his gifts. He explains that money is worthless apart from Christ, but it has great value when used for His sake. He writes,

> Money used to pad our securities and comforts is worthless. But when it is used for Christ's Kingdom, its investment power is infinitely greater than even the best bull market. Money used for Christ buys much more than Porsches, fur coats, Rolexes, big homes or nice retirements. It gives us greater delight in Jesus and spreads His mercy to others.[9]

In the next chapter, you will read the stories of some of God's great "mercy spreaders." And by the way . . . how much mercy are *you* spreading around?

4

Personal Stories
from Today's Christian Stewards

O LORD our God, all this abundance that we have prepared to build You
a house for Your holy name is from Your hand, and is all Your own.

—1 Chronicles 29:16 NKJV

CAN GOD TRUST YOU WITH FINANCIAL SUCCESS?

When I think about models of mature Christian stewardship, the
names Robert G. LeTourneau, Stanley Tam, Paul J. Meyer, and Truett
Cathy quickly come to mind. But I also think of Mr. Laurence Luce. I
met Mr. Luce at a church family camp when I was fifteen years old. It
was my joy to develop a friendship with him, and I have come to see
that he was one of the outstanding Christian stewards of the previous
century.

Laurence was the founder of Blue Bird Body Company, one of the
largest school bus manufacturers in the world. He and his wife, Helen,
were devoted followers of Christ. Their modest lifestyle and generous
giving to Christian higher education and world missions witnessed to
the lordship of Christ in their lives. Their oldest son, George, remembers a defining moment in his dad's life and in the history of Blue Bird.

The door to the Luces' home was always open to visiting evangel-
ists. One minister who stayed with them prayed for the success of the
bus company. George vividly recalls the minister's words in prayer:

"Lord, if you can trust Mr. Luce with financial success, I ask You to bless him with a prosperous business. If You can't, then I ask You to withhold that blessing."

"I had never heard a prayer quite like that before," said George, "and I don't know that I've heard anything since that expressed the same thought." But from that point on, his dad frequently referred to that prayer when faced with important decisions. It shaped the way he did business and lived his life.[1]

I saw first-hand the impact of Laurence Luce's stewardship as I served with two of the ministries he so generously supported. While he was one of the first biblical stewards I ever met, it has been my joy to meet hundreds of them through more than forty years in ministry with World Gospel Mission, Ohio Christian University, and EQUIP.

I thank God for the modern-day biblical stewards who are partnering with EQUIP to develop leaders to serve the growing, worldwide body of Christ. All of them faithfully use their possessions for His honor and glory. They are powerful examples of mature stewardship. Here is one of their stories:

Two Reasons for Success

In 1972, Joyce Eddy founded Habersham, a leading manufacturer of hand-painted furniture, in Clarksville, Georgia. Since its inception, the company has grown in sales and profits every year in an industry that has seen many manufacturers fold. In fact, while most furniture companies have closed plants and lost jobs to China, Habersham has flourished.

The story began when Joyce was a single mother of two sons. While operating a small antique nook above the local laundromat, a fire destroyed half of her shop. Right after that, her uninsured house also burned to the ground.

To bring in extra money while trying to recover from these double-whammy tragedies, Joyce began painting wooden cigar boxes and selling them as pocketbooks. An instant hit with customers, the boxes led

Joyce into a new venture as the forerunner of the current business.

One day, she spotted a large pile of wooden spools next to a local textile mill. An idea struck. She bought the spools for two cents apiece, worked her paintbrush magic on them, and turned them into decorative candleholders and towel racks.

"There are two reasons for our success.
The first one is the Lord and the second is the Lord."

—MATT EDDY, PRESIDENT OF HABERSHAM DESIGNS

Today the Habersham line ranges from occasional furniture to very expensive, cleverly designed armoires priced at thousands of dollars. Every piece of furniture is hand painted and signed by the artist—a dedication to craftsmanship that is at the core of the Habersham philosophy. But it is not the beautiful, hand-painted designs that are responsible for the company's widespread success. Joyce and her son Matt,[2] both devout Christians, are quick to state that a far higher calling guides them. Matt expresses it this way: "There are two reasons for our success. The first one is the Lord and the second is the Lord."[3]

I'll never forget my first visit with Matt Eddy in his office in the somewhat rustic two-story house that has been converted to Habersham's headquarters. After a few minutes of conversation, Matt guided me on a tour of the manufacturing plant, adjacent to the office building. Even though Matt walks with considerable difficulty due to a slowly crippling muscular disease, he was full of excitement as he greeted employee after employee and explained to me the art of producing superb furniture. Occasionally, Matt had to prod me to keep up with him because I could not resist lingering to admire the work of the skilled artisans who were transforming raw lumber into treasures of rare and exquisite beauty.

As Matt shared the Habersham story, I could tell that he and his mother are much more than successful entrepreneurs; they are mature biblical stewards. They understand that God is the owner of Habersham, and—as committed followers of Christ—they see the Great Commission, not furniture manufacturing, as their "business."

Back in his second-floor office, Matt turned to me and said, "We do what we do in order to invest in reaching the world for Christ." When I tried to thank Matt for his generous support of EQUIP, he interrupted me and said kindly but firmly, "No, I am the one who is thankful. I am grateful for the privilege of partnership with an organization that is strategically impacting the world for Christ."

Matt and I have had numerous opportunities for Christian fellowship and discussions about life in general. Each time, the conversation turns to the Great Commission. He is Great Commission–driven. Matt lives to invest in EQUIP, the *Jesus* Film Project, and other global endeavors that focus entirely on reaching the nations with the gospel of Jesus Christ.

When Matt heard the vision for Million Leaders Mandate, EQUIP's initiative to develop one million leaders to serve the universal body of Christ, he volunteered to serve as an associate trainer. Considering the challenges he faces walking even short distances, I must admit that I questioned the wisdom of his commitment to travel to the Philippines every six months for three years. The extremely long flights to the Far East are difficult for someone even in perfect health. To further complicate matters, he and his ministry partner, Rev. Greg Smith, had agreed to teach biblical leadership principles to pastors in Cebu City, requiring extra travel beyond Manila.

Matt and Greg have completed six rounds of conferences in the Philippines, pouring their lives into church leaders over a three-year period. It hasn't always been easy. At least once Matt has fallen while climbing the steps to the platform to teach a lesson. But he continues to rejoice that he can be involved in "multiplying effective leaders for the harvest fields." (Matt and Greg began teaching for EQUIP in a second nation in 2006, when Million Leaders Mandate was launched in Latin America.) He doesn't hesitate to give his all, because he recognizes that you can't outgive God.

You Can't Outgive God

More than any other factor in a person's formative years, family life forges character. In *Today Matters*, John Maxwell quotes Perry F. Webb on this critical element of childhood development: "The home . . . is the lens through which we get our first look at marriage and all the civic duties; it is the clinic where, by conversation and attitude, impressions are created with respect to sobriety and reverence; it is the school where lessons of truth or falsehood, honesty or deceit are learned, it is the mold which ultimately determines the structure of society."[4] In brief, home is where we learn our *values*. Home is also where we learn—and teach—stewardship.

Steve Miller, another one of our associate trainers, grew up in a home where stewardship was a priority. Since February 2003, this young businessman has taught leadership every six months in Jakarta, Indonesia. Recently I talked with Steve about his family, his business, and his faith.

Steve and his five siblings grew up in Holmes County, Ohio, in the heart of Amish country. His parents, both from Amish backgrounds, gave their hearts to Christ in early adulthood. His dad owned a sawmill, where all the children were taught very early in life how to work hard. Steve was the youngest of the family, but that did not exempt him from working at the mill. "I can remember stacking lumber when I was in the third grade," he told me. "I hated snow days, when our school was closed. It meant ten hours of hard work at the sawmill."

By age seven, Steve was showing early signs of entrepreneurship. In his early teens he bought and sold several products, earning enough money to pay cash for his first car. Because of his parents' teachings and example, he faithfully tithed his income from the first dime he earned at age seven.

In the early '80s, when Steve was in high school, his family went through one tragedy after another. One of his brothers nearly lost a hand in an incident at the mill. His oldest brother was killed in a logging accident. Then the sawmill was destroyed by fire, and the family struggled to survive financially. Steve will never forget his dad's strong faith during this difficult period. He remembers his father saying, "We don't understand all these things, but we know that God is faithful, and He will see us through victoriously." Steve added, "And God never failed us!"

While a freshman at Bible college in 1985, Steve earnestly prayed to discover God's perfect plan for his life. God responded by calling him to become a businessman. "As surely as God calls some people into pastoral ministry," he told me, "he also calls men and women into business."

At age nineteen, Steve felt God leading him to build wooden pallets for use in industry. Immediately he secured some extremely old, worn-out equipment and began to pursue his dream. From day one Steve prayed, "Dear God, I want to build a unique business that truly honors You. I honestly desire to create wealth for one purpose—to help advance Your kingdom." Steve later explained to me, "I clearly understood from the very start that the purpose of the business was for me to become a generous giver."

Steve is quick to say that God's Word is the foundation on which Millwood, Inc., has been built. He said recently, "Deuteronomy 8:18 reminds me that God is the source of our success. Malachi 3:10 and Luke 6:38 remind us to give faithfully and generously. We have learned that we simply cannot outgive God!" He explained, "When I read Malachi 3:10, I felt God challenging me to put His giving principles and promises to the test. I obeyed His Word, and God has opened the windows of heaven and poured out blessings and opportunities just as He promised.

"Our confidence in God's Word has been tested on a few occasions, especially in the early years of the company," Steve stated. "But faith is not faith until it is tested.

"God has never failed us," he concludes. "In nineteen years our company has grown from one tiny plant, full of used equipment, to

---

"God is the greatest giver in the universe,
and He won't let you out give Him."

—RANDY ALCORN, THE LAW OF REWARDS

---

eighteen modern manufacturing facilities across the Midwest. We now employ nearly one thousand people. Growth opportunities are too numerous to count." In 1996, God provided a business partner, Chip Trebilcock, who complements Steve's skills, shares his values, and understands God's purpose for the business. Steve has described his partner as one of God's special blessings.

There will always be challenges and trying times in life and in business, Steve warns. Personal and business growth are not without struggles. But he has learned the importance of walking every day by faith, because hardships, he believes, stretch our faith, take us outside our comfort zones, test our leadership skills, and remind us that we are dependent upon God.

Steve and his wife, Julie, have moved from being tithers to generous givers to biblical stewards. They now have the joy of supporting not only their local church, but also several compassionate ministries and international missionary work. They are especially delighted to partner generously with EQUIP, believing that leadership development is the key to a multiplied harvest of souls across the globe. Undoubtedly, one of their greatest joys is teaching their three young sons to be generous givers.

WHEN GIVING BECOMES BLISS

Dr. John C. Maxwell is known and loved by millions of people here in America and around the world. Because of his best-selling books and his monthly leadership lessons on CD, many leaders worldwide consider him their personal mentor. His older brother, Larry, in contrast, is not known for public ministry. But because of his generosity as a biblical steward, he, too, is having a global impact for God.

Larry is quiet and reserved but strong and focused. While relationally warm, he tends to be a man of few words. You will almost never see him on the platform or with a microphone, but behind the scenes he has major influence for the kingdom of God. And when Larry does speak, people listen.

Larry grew up in a Christian home in central Ohio. His parents, Melvin and Laura Maxwell, are two of the most authentic Christians I have ever met. Larry loved and respected his parents, but he did not make a commitment to Christ during his boyhood. Recently Larry told me that one day, when he was a high-school senior, his Grandpa Maxwell called him aside. Placing his hand on Larry's head, he said, "My son, God's hand is upon your life. You will one day become a successful businessman who will give generously to the cause of Christ." Larry admitted, "I truthfully didn't understand what he was saying until many years later."

Larry went on to college and also spent time in the Air Force. He married Anita Moats, a lovely young lady who also grew up under the guidance and care of godly parents.

At age twenty-six, in the mid-1960s, Larry tried to launch a career in business. He said, "I struggled financially for several years. While I didn't go into bankruptcy, I was surely broke most of the time." He added, "In those days I didn't have a personal relationship with Christ. However, I tithed my limited income out of a sense of duty that had been instilled in me by my parents' example . . . but I certainly found no joy in giving."

By 1977, the business was showing signs of growth. Larry and Anita moved to Florida to give leadership to the slowly expanding business. Shortly thereafter, Larry gave his heart to Christ. As Larry grew in his faith, his attitude toward giving changed. He no longer gave out of a sense of duty. Giving became a joy! The discipleship journey paralleled his journey as a biblical steward.

The business grew rapidly, and as it did, Larry quickly learned that God honors generosity. Over the years, Larry became involved in real estate development, nursing homes, and banking. Not only did Larry and Anita give freely from their personal income, but they also began to give liberally from their business profits. Then, to maximize their contributions and teach their children the joy of giving, they created a charitable family foundation whose mission, based on God's Word (Matt. 25:34–36), is to serve those who are needy, both spiritually and physically.

Larry has been invited to serve on the boards of key evangelical ministries, where he has offered not only valuable business counsel but financial resources. In 1996, Larry joined his brother, John, and a few other Christian leaders to launch the ministry of EQUIP. As one of the founding board members, Larry's wisdom and business acumen helped shepherd EQUIP through its infancy. "EQUIP has become one of the special joys of my life," he says. "What a blessing to invest generously in this ministry that is having such a huge impact worldwide. I thank God for His blessings upon EQUIP, a ministry that is now training hundreds of thousands of church leaders around the globe." Larry added, "I firmly believe that effective leaders must be developed if the nations are to be reached for Christ. I consider gifts to train and resource Christian leaders as strategic investments that give multiplied eternal dividends."

Larry continues to provide wise counsel and generous monetary support as a very active member of EQUIP's governing board. John Hull, president of EQUIP, stated recently, "Larry is a wonderful blessing and encouragement to me. I often turn to him for advice when facing major decisions. What a wonderful privilege to have this wise man walking beside me." John Maxwell adds, "Other than my wife, Margaret, Larry is my best friend and most trusted advisor."

Larry commented, "I have been blessed with more than enough. As I grow older, I weigh more and more decisions in light of eternity. I now live to lay up treasures in heaven. As quickly as possible, I am changing my earthly currency into heavenly currency as I invest in Great Commission work."

KEEP YOUR HANDS OPEN

Don Meyer, president of Baillie Lumber in New York, grew up in a tithing home. Early on, he, like his father, faithfully gave the first 10 percent of his paychecks to the Lord's work. But when he went into the lumber business in 1957, he didn't carry his giving pattern with him. There were very little profits to tithe from, he rationalized. In time, though, he decided to tithe on his business as well.

In the early days with the company, Don received a call from the development officer of Wheaton College, asking for a donation. Assuring Don that God would provide for their needs with or without *his* contributions, the older and wiser gentleman began to talk to Don about the blessings that come from giving. He then warned Don that as his business grew, he would likely be tempted to hold on tightly to his money. He challenged the young businessman to open his hands and to keep them open, emphasizing that we are merely the stewards of God's money.

In the early '70s Japan was building four-story bowling alleys, and in a period of nine months, the Japanese doubled the price of hardwoods. About the same time, there was a furniture explosion. Don promptly saw large amounts of revenue pouring into his company. And, yes, he *was* tempted to close his hands and concentrate on growing his business even bigger. But then he remembered the counsel he had received years earlier. He chose to open his hands, and he generously gave his profits back to the Lord.

Don has practiced the lesson well, and eventually he got to the point of capping his net worth. At this point, he says, "I decided to de-accumulate." Don and his wife determined a salary they would live on, and all of the profits above that would go directly to Christian ministry. More than once God has given them money they never expected, and with open hands they've given it right back to Him—it's all His anyway!

HUGS

Ray Lyne, founder and president of Lifestyle Giving, Inc., is one of my dearest friends. Ray probably understands and articulates biblical stewardship concepts better than anyone I have met in more than forty years of Christian ministry. He has devoted most of his adult life to helping God's people understand and practice Christian steward-ship. I was with Ray on one occasion when someone asked him, "Just what is it you do?" Ray replied, "I am into hugs." Then he proceeded to explain that every Christian should be interested in three special hugs. His mission in life is to help Christians live as biblical stewards so they will not forfeit these hugs.

The first hug is undoubtedly the most important. It is a huge hug from God the Father when we reach the end of our journey on planet earth. This hug will be accompanied by the Father's commendation, "Well done, good and faithful servant" (Matt. 25:21 NKJV).

I grew up in southern Georgia in a "hugging family." Hugs from loving parents, siblings, and friends were abundant. Winnie and I have built a home filled with hugs. But I am determined to receive the ulti-mate hug—the "well done" embrace from my heavenly Father when I complete life's journey!

The second hug has the potential of being repeated countless times. It is the hug received from one whose life has been impacted by the gospel as a result of the biblical steward's faithfulness and generos-ity. As we walk the streets of heaven, folks we've never met will come to us with loving embraces and words of gratitude. "Thank you for investing in the Great Commission," they will say. "I'm here because of *your* obedience."

The third hug can also be repeated many times—by our children. It comes from leaving a legacy of stewardship in their lives. It involves effectively modeling generosity in such a way that they, too, become generous givers. Then, rather than fighting over the stuff we leave behind, they will continue to hug one another long after the estate has been settled.[5]

LEARNING STEWARDSHIP BY EXAMPLE

Alan Gotthardt also talks about the steward's children in his very practical and helpful book, *The Eternity Portfolio*. "We all know that children learn by example," he says. "This is particularly true with giving;

"Children learn by example. This is particularly true with giving; children of generous givers become generous givers."

—ALAN GOTTHARDT

---

children of generous givers become generous givers, often because of the example they witnessed growing up."[6]

Alan explains that our daily living reveals just how much of the Bible we really believe. He reminds us that we should not expect our children to believe what they do not see consistently in our lives. "A faithful life," he says, "is the best platform for teaching others." He argues that the faithful steward "radiates the joy of the generous life in such a way as to be unbelievably attractive to others."[7]

Author Todd Duncan, one of our partners and founder of The Duncan Group, frequently affirms that it was his parents' example that shaped his core values and instilled in him a desire to make a difference that will count for eternity. "From the age of 12," he wrote in a letter to EQUIP, "I have been impacted by the importance of getting the message of salvation to every corner of the world. My parents were a model of international evangelism as I watched them take trip after trip to get the Word of Christ into the thirsty hearts and souls of people."[8] Todd has told me on several occasions that what he saw in his parents laid the foundation for his life today—a life that passionately seeks to be Spirit-led at all times. He further stated in his letter:

> The Holy Spirit has laid [a] sense of urgency on my heart to partner financially with EQUIP . . . to be a part of the Living Legacy Group because I [know] that through God's blessings on me and my family, we [can] be an even bigger blessing on others . . . By making it possible for over 1,000,000 leaders to learn how to lead . . . millions more will [come to] know the joy of having Christ as their Savior.[9]

Todd understands that building the kingdom of God is about raising more than money. It's also about raising leaders who can teach others the *joy of giving*.

5

The Joy of Giving

Let each one give as he purposes in his heart, not grudgingly or of necessity; for God loves a cheerful giver. And God is able to make all grace abound toward you, that you, always having all sufficiency in all things, may have an abundance for every good work.

—2 Corinthians 9:7–8 NKJV

Imagine giving so liberally of your wealth, time, and talents that the Lord actually had to beg you to *stop*. The book of Exodus records an amazing story of a people so generous that they had to be *ordered* to stop giving.

Moses spoke to all the congregation of the children of Israel, saying, "This is the thing which the LORD commanded . . . 'Take from among you an offering to the LORD. Whoever is of a *willing* heart, let him bring . . . gold, silver, and bronze; blue, purple, and scarlet thread, fine linen, and goats' hair; ram skins dyed red, badger skins, and acacia wood; oil for the light, and spices for the anointing oil and for the sweet incense; onyx stones, and stones to be set in the ephod and in the breastplate.

"'All who are gifted artisans among you shall come and make all that the LORD has commanded: the tabernacle, its tent . . . the ark and its poles, with the mercy seat, and the veil of the covering; the table . . . , all its utensils, and the showbread; also the lampstand . . . and the oil for the light; the incense altar . . . the anointing oil, the sweet incense, and . . . the garments of ministry.'" . . . And all the congregation . . . departed from the presence of Moses.

Then everyone came whose heart was stirred, and everyone whose spirit was *willing*, and they brought the LORD's offering . . . Both men and women, as many as had a *willing* heart, . . . brought earrings and nose rings, rings and necklaces, all jewelry of gold . . . And every man, with whom was found blue, purple, and scarlet thread, fine linen, goats' hair, red skins of rams, and badger skins, brought them. Everyone who offered an offering of silver or bronze brought the LORD's offering. And everyone with whom was found acacia wood for any work of the service, brought it. All the women who were gifted artisans spun yarn with their hands, and brought what they had spun . . . And all the women whose hearts stirred with wisdom spun yarn of goats' hair. The rulers brought onyx stones, and the stones to be set in the ephod and in the breastplate, and spices and oil for the light, for the anointing oil, and for the sweet incense. The children of Israel brought a freewill offering to the LORD, all the men and women whose hearts were *willing* to bring material for all kinds of work . . .

Then Moses called . . . every gifted artisan in whose heart the LORD had put wisdom, everyone whose heart was stirred, to come and do the work. And they received from Moses all the offering which the children of Israel had brought . . . So they continued bringing to him freewill offerings every morning.

Then all the craftsmen . . . [said], "The people bring much more than enough for the service of the work which the LORD commanded us to do." So Moses gave a commandment, and they caused it to be proclaimed throughout the camp, saying, "Let neither man nor woman do any more work for the offering of the sanctuary." And the people were restrained from bringing, for the material they had was sufficient for all the work to be done—indeed *too much*. (Ex. 35:4–36:7 NKJV, emphasis added.)

I don't look for the Lord to issue a "cease and desist" anytime soon where our giving is concerned, but let's explore some interesting questions that this story raises: Why do you think God's people were so willing of heart? Why did they give so generously to His work? I believe it's because they had already discovered a most sacred truth: there's *joy in generosity*.

JOY IN GENEROSITY

There are many folks today who maintain that the only joy to be found is in accumulating money. Others would argue that joy is really found in the stuff money can buy. Through my many years of involvement

---

"My father used to say, 'You can spend a lot of time making money. The tough time comes when you have to give it away properly.' How to give something back, that's the tough part in life."

—LEE IACOCCA,

FORMER CHAIRMAN OF CHRYSLER CORPORATION

---

with Christian ministry, I have established friendships with men and women from almost every socioeconomic stratum, ranging from the very poor to the extremely rich. And I have observed repeatedly that, whatever their income, those who are the most generous in their giving seem to be the happiest. In fact, every Christian steward I know tells me that his or her greatest joy comes from giving.

Paul J. Meyer, a mature Christian steward who has invested millions in God's work, declares, "No joy matches my joy from giving." Paul often tells successful marketplace leaders, "You thought it was fun making it. Well, you don't know what fun is until you start giving it away." He adds, "I feel guilty because I feel so hilariously happy today and explosive with joy."[1] Paul is "explosive with joy" because he is using his assets to fulfill, not *his* plan, but God's. And what a wonderful plan God has designed:

- He provides all of our resources.
- His Word guides us in how to manage those resources wisely for maximum kingdom impact.
- We get to experience the joy of being faithful and generous stewards.
- We can partner with God in His Great Commission plan to reach a lost world.
- We can spend eternity with Him and those we have helped to reach with His salvation message.

Randy Alcorn may have stated it best: "Of investments they say, 'If it sounds too good to be true, it probably is.' But in the case of the amazing return we can get on investments in God's Kingdom, it is true. God Himself guarantees it."[2]

In Part I we have discussed *personal* stewardship, how we can use our personal resources for building the kingdom of God. We can do so much for His kingdom when we, as individuals, give.

But perhaps you've heard it said that "there's power in numbers." What if, instead of giving *alone*, we pooled our resources with those of *others*? What if we gave in *partnership* with others? Would that make a difference?

In Part II we will discuss the purpose, principles, and power of partnership, and how we can use partnership to accomplish God's dreams—*together*!

Part II

Partnership:
Accomplishing God's Dreams
Together

There isn't a single person in the world that can make a pencil. The wood may have come from a forest in Washington, the graphite from a mine in South America, and the eraser from a Malaysian rubber plantation. Thousands of people cooperate to make a pencil.

—Milton Friedman

On New Year's Day in 1939, William Hewlett and David Packard formalized their partnership with a coin toss to decide the company name. It wasn't easy starting a company during the Depression, but Hewlett and Packard shared two basic sentiments that ensured their success: (1) admiration for individual creativity and initiative and (2) trust in their employees. Their commitment to making these two attitudes part of their management approach catapulted their partnership into one of the most influential companies of the twentieth century.[1]

In the business world, *partnership* means a legal contract entered into by two or more persons, in which each agrees to furnish a part of the capital and labor for a business enterprise, and by which each shares a fixed portion of the profits and losses.[2]

The Hewlett-Packard team was unique in how they facilitated partnerships. The essence of their radical philosophy was that the company's most important resource was their employees' brainpower. Based on that conviction, management formed a partnership with their workers. They also developed partnerships with each of their customers. No HP customer was to be treated as simply a buyer. Hewlett-Packard's goal was to view customers as *partners* and to develop a long-term association with every single one. Together they could solve business problems. The customer provided the challenges, and HP created the technology to meet them.[3]

In the context of the Christian community, partnership is used in a much broader and less formal context. It typically means simple cooperation between two or more individuals or organizations, usually to enhance ministry efficiency and/or effectiveness. Partnerships may be entered into with formal documents, but in most cases they are informal, often based on a conversation, a handshake, and perhaps an e-mail to summarize the agreement. They are not typically formed on paper. They are shaped in the hearts of spiritually mature men and women who trust one another and desire to impact the kingdom of God. Ministry partners commit their very best to each other for as long as it takes to accomplish a mutually agreed-upon mission. In this way, partnerships take a shared vision from a dream to a reality.

I have seen far too much competition and duplication in the global missionary enterprise. As such, I firmly believe that partnership is vital to the achievement of the Great Commission. Many wonderful examples prove it. The Co-Mission effort to impact Russia for Christ is an outstanding illustration of ministry partnership. The *Jesus* Film Project has effectively established partnerships with a variety of denominations and organizations.

In the following chapters I will take a look at *partnership* as a core value at EQUIP. You'll see how strategic partnerships are enabling a comparatively small organization to develop millions of effective leaders around the world—in other words, to raise *more than money*.

6

The Purpose and Principles of Partnership

Two are better than one, because they have a good reward for their labor. For if they fall, one will lift up his companion. But woe to him who is alone when he falls, for he has no one to help him up.

—Ecclesiastes 4:9–10 NKJV

Moses said . . . "I am not able to bear all these people alone, because the burden is too heavy for me" . . . So the LORD said . . . "Gather to Me seventy men . . . I will take of the Spirit that is upon you and will put the same upon them; and they shall bear the burden of the people with you, that you may not bear it yourself alone."

—Numbers 11:11–17 NKJV

GOD-SIZED DREAMS

"Nothing of significance was ever achieved by an individual acting alone,"[1] writes Dr. John C. Maxwell, EQUIP's founder. In John's live leadership conferences, he often asks his audience to give him the name of anyone who single-handedly accomplished something significant. On one occasion an attendee offered the name Charles Lindbergh, the famous aviator who flew solo across the Atlantic Ocean. John immediately reminded his listeners that even though the plane was flown by just *one* man, *several* wealthy St. Louis individuals provided the financial backing for the flight—which Lindbergh achieved in an aircraft designed by a *group* of engineers.

In February 2005, Jeff Gordon, four-time NASCAR driving champion, won the Daytona 500 race for the third time. In a postrace interview he said, "I drove the car, but hundreds of people helped to put this car in victory lane." He then thanked the car's owner, the crew chief, engineers, mechanics, machinists, the pit crew, thousands of employees of his financial sponsors, and many others. Indeed, countless hands touched that car on its way to the championship of the Great American Race.

I am convinced that when individuals work together, the likelihood of significant accomplishment is greatly enhanced. The same is true when organizations cooperate. Based on this belief, EQUIP has formed numerous partnerships with individuals, local churches, denominations, associations, interdenominational agencies, and indigenous overseas ministries in our effort to find, raise up, train, and resource millions of leaders to reach the nations for Christ.

We believe partnerships should be formed for the following reasons:

1. *Effectiveness*: The greater the effectiveness, the greater the results.
2. *Efficiency*: The greater the efficiency, the better the use of resources.
3. *Empowerment*: The greater the empowerment, the greater the mobilization of people, gifts, and abilities.

Ministry Partners

We apply the partnership principle to all of our development efforts at EQUIP by seeing those who give to EQUIP as ministry *partners*. In 2003, we launched the Million Leaders Mandate, a global initiative to develop one million effective leaders to reach the nations with the gospel. Using the strategy of multiplication, we asked our financial partners who love to teach, to serve as associate trainers. In less than three years, over two hundred of our donors have volunteered to travel overseas every six months over a three-year period to teach biblical leadership principles to thousands of leaders. They have traveled from Manila to Cairo, from Cape Town to Moscow, from New Delhi to La Paz. And the associate trainers pay their own travel expenses, in addition to their very generous regular giving to EQUIP. We endeavor to serve them as true partners in ministry through a variety of means:

1. Quarterly, we offer a special workshop, using EQUIP's international leadership curriculum, in which we train them in effectively communicating in a cross-cultural context.
2. International partners assist our associate trainers with logistical arrangements (ground transportation, lodging, etc.) while they are serving overseas.
3. Country coordinators ensure that all of the details for the two-day leadership conferences are handled with excellence. This involves not only providing an adequate venue and qualified interpreters but also distributing the workbooks and other resources. The country coordinators are also responsible for recruiting influential conference attendees who are both eager to learn biblical leadership principles and willing to individually mentor at least twenty-five other Christian leaders.
4. We provide leadership books. We also offer leadership lessons and teaching helps on CDs and via the Internet.
5. We provide timely updates by phone, e-mail, our Web site, videos, and newsletters of ministry progress and prayer requests.
6. We listen to our partners and encourage input and feedback. We are always eager to hear from our associate trainers as well as our other prayer and financial partners.

We also apply the partnership principle to our international leadership curriculum, both in its creation and its worldwide dissemination. While the Bible is the foundation of our curriculum and the writings of John Maxwell provide most of the content, Crown

Financial Ministries, Global Focus, LaRed Business Network, and Ken Blanchard's Lead Like Jesus ministry have also contributed materials. International Christian Publishers translates, prints, and ships millions of EQUIP workbooks to training sites worldwide.

Our volunteer associate trainers are placing the curriculum into the heads, hands, and hearts of thousands upon thousands of certified

---

If you can achieve your dream all alone,
your dream is very likely not from God.

---

national trainers globally who represent scores of denominations, fellowships, associations, and agencies. Each certified national trainer uses the curriculum to mentor twenty-five other leaders. In Indonesia alone, more than 160 denominations are participating in the Million Leaders Mandate.

The fact that we need one another is a key reason for partnership. I am convinced that a God-given ministry vision is always too large for us to accomplish alone. No individual or organization possesses all of the talents and resources necessary to accomplish the task. Quite honestly, if you can achieve your dream all alone, your dream is very likely not from God. God-sized dreams require the help of both God *and* others.

WIN-WIN RELATIONSHIPS

It is in partnerships that we develop win-win relationships. What any individual or organization can do alone is so terribly small when compared to what can be accomplished by working together. The most rewarding relationships are always partnerships. This is true in business, in marriage, and in ministry.[2] But before you can even begin to reap the *rewards* of partnership, you must first gain an understanding of the *principles* of partnership.

The Principles of Partnership

Through the years, partnerships have been formed for a variety of reasons. In 1837, William Procter, candle maker, and James Gamble, soap maker, pooled their limited resources and individual talents to form a joint venture that eventually became one of the most successful businesses in America.[3] In the 1930s, entertainer Bud Abbott met burlesque comic Lou Costello, and together they formed a comedy team that became legendary.[4] There are countless other duos in the business world and entertainment field that have achieved colossal success while working together. Many of them were unsuccessful as solo performers.

The Bible tells the story of the ministry partnership between David and Jonathan. It is a story of sacrificial partnership for the sake of the kingdom, not for the benefit of one person. It is interesting to note that even though Prince Jonathan had every right to ascend to the throne, he used his influence to promote David as the next king of

---

"Partnership is a crucial part of God's design for us."

— AUTHOR UNKNOWN

Israel. And David clearly valued his partnership with Jonathan. The following excerpt from *Leadership Promises for Every Day* describes how this historic partnership strengthened David's future leadership:

1. It helped others see the contribution of every man's gift.
2. It reminded everyone that God was the true source of every good gift.
3. It promoted goodwill in potential allies.
4. It enabled David to prepare for the future and make friends all over Israel.
5. It developed a nationwide value of mutual benefit and good faith.[5]

KEY PRINCIPLES

As I have examined many successful partnerships, I've discovered some key principles that I'd like to share with you:

1. *Partnerships are about multiplication.* Partnerships multiply skills, energy, creativity, resources, and results.

2. *Partnerships must be based on trust.* To establish and maintain trust, each partner must exhibit both competence and flawless character. Once trust exists, often a handshake will mark the launch of a partnership. Integrity must remain at the heart of any partnership that lasts.

3. *Partnerships are formed to accomplish a shared goal or mission.* They should meet real needs in the lives of the people they serve.

4. *Partnerships are always a process.* Building trust and establishing structures and guidelines for ministry together will not happen instantly.

5. *Partnerships are formed around the strengths of each partner.* One partner complements the other, bringing needed expertise and/or resources to the table.

6. *Partnerships have conditions.* Effective partnerships require long-term commitment, open and regular communication, generosity, flexibility, and a focus on the big picture. The solidity of a partnership is conditional upon a dedication to these issues.

BIG-PICTURE THINKING

Big-picture thinking is crucial. Partners focus on opportunities, not obstacles.

They are empowered by possibilities and refuse to be derailed by problems. The priority of meeting real needs overpowers pet projects and personal preferences. Logos and egos are laid aside for the sake of the Kingdom. Principles, not personalities, guide partnerships. A spirit of competition is rejected. The workload of each partner must be perceived as balanced and fair.

David Gage is a mediator and psychologist who provides strategies for making partnerships work. During a visit to the University of Massachusetts' Family Business Center, "Gage recounted an anecdote about ice cream magnates Ben and Jerry, early in their career. Jerry was feeling resentful that he was stuck stirring cookies into ice cream mixes through the night, while Ben was home sleeping—until he remembered that Ben had to get up at 5 a.m. and drive the new flavor around."[6] Jerry, at first indignant, was okay once he looked at the *big picture.* When he did, he realized that what Ben was doing at 5 a.m. *complemented* his work on the graveyard shift. Effective partnerships focus on learning how to complement each other in the mission. That goes for ministry partnerships too.

In short, ministry partners must do *five* things exceedingly well:

1. Consecrate—commit to God and one another.
2. Concentrate—focus on the mission.
3. Communicate—connect frequently. Silence, not distance, separates us.
4. Cultivate—invest in the relationship and learn to serve each other.
5. Celebrate—rejoice with one another, always sharing credit for the victory.

Only by committing to these five essential practices can you and your partners begin to engage in world-impacting ministry. Once you do, you will soon discover the *power of partnership.*

7

The Power of Partnership

If two lie down together, they will keep warm; but how can one be warm
alone? Though one may be overpowered . . . , two can withstand . . . and
a threefold cord is not quickly broken.

—Ecclesiastes 4:11–12 NKJV

In 1996, Dr. John C. Maxwell and several other Christian leaders
founded a nonprofit organization for the purpose of raising up, training, and equipping international leaders for Great Commission ministry. They called this organization EQUIP.

In 1998, in an EQUIP Founders Club gathering in Atlanta, Dr.
Maxwell shared a devotional with several of EQUIP's financial partners. "Partnership in ministry is powerful," he told them. He then gave
them six reasons why:

1. *Partnership multiplies ministry effectiveness.* It eliminates or
    minimizes duplication, competition, and waste.
2. *Partnership unifies the body of Christ.* It requires us to focus
    on God's agenda, not our own.
3. *Partnership purifies the motives of leaders.* We can't take the
    credit for accomplishments. God receives the credit.
4. *Partnership testifies to the world.* Jesus' prayer in John 17 is
    answered.

5. *Partnership intensifies our commitment to one another.* It tears down fences that prevent unity in the body of Christ.

6. *Partnership satisfies the heart of God.* It binds us together in a relationship in which we unselfishly give our best to the other. It is the "more excellent way" in action. (See 1 Corinthians 12:31 and following, NKJV.)

Partnership Reflects God's Nature

On an airplane flight several weeks later, I asked John to elaborate on the six statements he made about partnership. He immediately called my attention to the seventeenth chapter of the Gospel of John. As we discussed our Savior's prayer for the oneness of His followers, I realized that ministry partnership is consistent with the very nature of our God, who desires relationship with His people and a spirit of oneness within the family of God.

In 2002, John Maxwell shared with the EQUIP administrative team his dream to train at least one million international Christian leaders by 2008. That goal was realized in 2006, but by then the vision had grown to *five* million additional leaders by 2012, and *fifty* million by 2020. When we looked at the immense size of the dream and the very small size of our team, we immediately knew that forming partnerships was the only way to see this dream accomplished.

As we began the search for partners who could offer the expertise that we lacked, it became clear that organizations who understand partnership are focused on God's agenda, not their own. Their motives are pure. The fulfillment of the Great Commission, not the promotion of their institutions, is their reason for existence. We began to pray that God would lead us to many such ministries.

International Christian Publishers became one of our first global partners. ICP is the publisher and distributor of millions of copies of *Book of Hope* worldwide. Because of our partnership, our leadership workbooks will be placed in the hands of tens of thousands of leaders from scores of nations, in their own languages, in more than two hundred international conferences this year. We are the writers and developers of quality leadership curriculum; they are the translators, printers, shippers, and intercontinental distributors. Our partnership is crucial to the success of the Million Leaders Mandate.

In January 2003, International Christian Ministries (ICM) agreed to oversee all the activities of EQUIP and the Million Leaders Mandate

---

"Partnership is an attitude before it becomes an action."

—TIM ELMORE

---

on the continent of Africa. ICM had already been conducting conferences across this vast continent for years, but they needed leadership curriculum. We, on the other hand, needed an organization that already had a network of individuals and organizations that could handle the myriad of logistical details involved in training successful leaders in every region of Africa. Within three years of officially launching our partnership, we were able to provide biblical leadership training and resources for more than 400,000 African leaders. What's more exciting is that this number can only increase, because we are regularly adding new sites across the African continent.

David Sobrepena pastors one of the largest churches in the Philippines. He was one of the first international leaders to enter into partnership with EQUIP. David has used his influence to enlist the cooperation of the evangelical alliance in his country and to build a coalition of churches, denominations, and agencies to participate in the Million Leaders Mandate project in that part of the world. As a result of his able leadership, in three years MLM trained more than 226,000 Filipino Christian leaders, and the total will continue to rise. Many of them are taking the leadership training to other Asian nations; one leader, for example, is teaching and mentoring 180 pastors in Vietnam.

Because of David's influence, John Maxwell and several of us on the EQUIP team were invited in 2003 to Manila to meet with the president of the Philippines, Mrs. Gloria Macapagal-Arroyo. Likewise, David paved the way for Dr. Maxwell to speak for the National Day of Prayer in the Philippines in 2004.

We have established similar partnerships with key pastors and churches in nation after nation in Asia, Africa, Europe, and Latin America. In the region known as the "Arab World," the largest evangelical church, located in Cairo, Egypt, has opened the door for EQUIP to provide biblical leadership coaching and materials for key church leaders in Southwest Asia and Northern Africa. It was the influence of our Egyptian partners that secured our access to Iraq to train leaders shortly after the fall of Saddam Hussein. This Cairo church has now provided a very sharp young leader from their own staff to serve with EQUIP in handling the prearrangements for our conferences around the world.

THE "SNOWBALL EFFECT"

My wife and I recently spent eight weeks visiting our ministry partners in several nations of the Asia Pacific region. We were based in Singapore, where we were hosted by Mike and Joyce Griffin and the staff of Equipping Leaders for Asia, a nonprofit ministry founded by Mike.

Mike came to Malaysia some thirty years ago as a Peace Corps volunteer. While serving in Asia, he met the lovely Malaysian Chinese lady who would become his wife. He also gave his heart to Christ.

Mike started a business in Indonesia and later in India. Through the years he developed exceptional skills as a corporate trainer. But as Mike grew in the Lord, he came to realize that he needed to devote more of his time and financial resources to the Lord's work.

Mike searched for a way to use his training skills in a cause that would advance the fulfillment of the Great Commission. In January

2003, while on a business trip in Mumbai, India, Mike learned that John Maxwell was in the city to launch the Million Leaders Mandate project in India. Mike decided to attend.

When Mike arrived at the conference, he and I met in the hallway. I am convinced that it was no accident. We began a conversation about EQUIP and our vision and strategy to develop a million effective

---

Snowball effect: A figurative term for a process that starts from an initial state of small significance and builds upon itself, becoming larger.[1]

Christian leaders around the world. Immediately Mike knew that he had found the mission in which he would use his expertise and invest his resources.

Without asking for anything from EQUIP except permission to use the curriculum, Mike volunteered to take the MLM training to as many nations of Asia as possible. Within a few months he had prepared a team of forty Asian associate trainers who would travel throughout the continent and teach the MLM curriculum. Today they are systematically training Christian leaders in China, India, Malaysia, Indonesia, Vietnam, Cambodia, Sri Lanka, Bangladesh, Nepal, Mongolia, New Zealand, Australia, Thailand, Laos, Myanmar, Borneo, Kazakhstan, and Singapore. Mike is generously and joyfully investing thousands of dollars to train key leaders in Southeast Asia.

Now that I know Mike well, I have renamed him Mr. Generosity. Seldom, if ever, have I met anyone so generous. I know no one who finds greater joy in giving to help others.

While in Asia, I met many of the superb associate trainers who were raised up by Mike Griffin and his ELA staff. Let me share the story of just one of them, a Singaporean Chinese brother I'll call Joseph for security reasons. For many years Joseph was a high-level executive with a major multinational corporation, overseeing the Asia Pacific region. He is also a key layman in his local church in Singapore.

A couple of years ago, reading Bob Buford's book, *Half Time*, led Joseph to devote more time and finances to ministry. He resigned from his corporate position and started his own consulting firm in order to free up time for the Lord's work. About that time he met Mike Griffin and learned about EQUIP and Million Leaders Mandate. Joseph became an associate trainer and now devotes much of his time to teaching MLM curriculum in several nations of the region.

In a breakfast conversation in Singapore, Joseph told me about his involvement with MLM. He is teaching leadership to more than four hundred leaders in Nepal. He has already taken them through four of the workbooks. He reported that MLM training has brought the churches in Nepal together for the first time ever. Virtually all of the two hundred Nepali churches are being impacted by EQUIP materials. Recently, using contacts through his former company, he has begun training Christian leaders in Australia. He is also teaching approximately one hundred leaders in Sri Lanka, a nation torn by ethnic strife and violence.

In Vietnam, where large gatherings are forbidden by the government, he is taking fifteen of the very top pastors in the nation through the EQUIP training. They are in turn coaching hundreds of others throughout the nation. One of Joseph's trainees had only fifteen people attending his house church two years ago but now leads a network of fifty thousand people and is taking the MLM training to all his leaders. This Vietnamese brother has been miraculously delivered several times from the hands of the secret police. The police fear him now because they have come to believe that he has special power from another world. They are afraid to harm him.

Joseph will soon begin teaching MLM curriculum to Christian marketplace leaders in Vietnam. And all of this has happened because of the vision of one man named Mike Griffin. Mike has been just like a rolling ball of snow, gaining momentum the farther he goes! His influence continues to affect his continent. Mike found Christ in Asia; now he is investing his assets and abilities to bring Asia to Christ.

DIVERSITY IN PARTNERSHIPS

Our list of ministry partners is long, ranging from very influential local churches overseas to indigenous national organizations to denominational and independent mission agencies. Dr. A. F. Pinto and Pastor David Mohan in India, Dr. Niko Nyotorahardjo in Indonesia, Pastor Sunday Adelaja in Ukraine, Pastor Misal Arsenal in Honduras, HCJB Global, Compassion International, WMIT Radio, Equipping Leaders for Asia (ELA), BEEWorld, Far East Broadcasting (FEBC), JMM World Outreach, and Strategic China Initiative (SCI) are just a few of the highly influential leaders and ministries that are working with us to train thousands of international Christian leaders.

And, of course, none of this could happen without our faithful prayer and financial partners. These generous, biblical stewards are providing the funding for millions of notebooks and other leadership resources. Many of them are serving as volunteer associate trainers, touching the lives of multitudes of leaders in world regions that are strategic to the completion of the Great Commission.

I wish I had the time and space to share all of their stories, but I can mention only a few. They represent a vanguard of servant-leaders who are changing the world as they invest their time and financial resources in training, equipping, and encouraging godly leaders to reach the nations with the gospel. In a phrase, they are *raising more than money*.

David Mimms is the president of Mimms Enterprises, one of the largest commercial real estate holders in the Atlanta area. When David committed to give generously to EQUIP and the Million Leaders Mandate, he had more than money in mind. He immediately challenged his pastor to join him as a volunteer associate trainer. They are now teaching the EQUIP leadership curriculum every six months in Ethiopia. Some of the leaders they are training in Addis Ababa are now taking the leadership instruction and resources to pastors in neighboring Sudan, a nation that daily endures unbelievable suffering.

Several times each year, David hosts a networking luncheon in the dining room of his company's headquarters. He brings in business associates and other friends and shares the EQUIP partnership opportunity. Many of them have committed to "the leadership journey" with EQUIP. Among them are David's father, Malon, who founded the company, and his uncle, Tom Mimms, an associate trainer in England.

Gary Ott leads a company in Marion, Indiana, that owns and operates nursing homes. Gary is one of our associate trainers in the Philippines. Shortly after one of his trips to Manila, he met George Clinton, a successful businessman from Richmond, Indiana. The story Gary shared about EQUIP was so compelling that George immediately contacted me, requesting additional information. Today, George and Vicki Clinton are two of our most generous partners, and George has taught leadership in Kenya every six months since 2004. He describes his service in Kenya as the most fulfilling and rewarding experience of his life. "EQUIP has given me purpose in life," he adds, "and my leadership abilities and communication skills are growing rapidly."

One of our unique partnerships is with Blue Ridge Broadcasting, an affiliate of the Billy Graham Evangelistic Association. Blue Ridge owns and operates nonprofit, Christian radio stations in North Carolina. In 2002, Tom Atema, then director of Blue Ridge Broadcasting, offered EQUIP a couple of days each year on his stations to raise funds for a special international project. In February 2003, EQUIP's president, John Hull, and Tom shared with the radio audience the opportunity to train leaders in the Middle East. The response was overwhelming. Tom immediately volunteered to serve as one of our associate trainers in Beirut, Lebanon. The annual radio fundraiser is now in its fifth year and continues to be a huge success. Tom has become one of our most effective trainers, teaching in Lebanon,

Egypt, and India. In 2005, Tom and his listeners provided the funds for training the underground house-church leaders in China. Tom became EQUIP's vice president of strategic partnerships in January 2006. Later in that same year he also became vice president of international ministries.

Rev. Phillip Knight, a former missionary to East Africa, is now the president of the Congregational Methodist Churches, an evangelical denomination with churches in the southeastern United States. Phil is now challenging all of his member churches to make EQUIP their primary partner in world mission outreach. Their largest church is near Griffin, Georgia, and is pastored by Dr. Benny Tate. Benny and his congregation invest generously in EQUIP and underwrite all the travel expenses for Phil to serve as an associate trainer in two Kenyan cities. In addition to Phil, Jerry Jones, director of world missions for the CMC, serves as an associate trainer in Namibia and Ecuador. As do many of our partners, CMC pastors attend forums and roundtables hosted by EQUIP for the purpose of adding value and blessing to our ministry partners. These interactive events are both informational and inspirational.

One of our rapidly growing partnerships is with Rev. Billy Hornsby and the Association of Related Churches (ARC). This association of churches is committed to providing guidance and resources for church planters. They are aggressively and effectively establishing new churches across our nation. Billy and the leaders of ARC challenge all member churches to become partners with EQUIP. Chris Hodges, Stovall Weems, Joe Champion, Dino Rizzo, Greg Surratt, Danny Chambers, Mike Ware, Rick and Randy Bezet, Troy Shaw, Phillip Carter, Matt Fry, Rob Ketterling, Phil Stern and many others of our key partners and associate trainers are members of ARC. One ARC church plant in the Atlanta area started giving monthly to EQUIP even before their first service was held.

Dr. John Hull, president of EQUIP, has frequently commented that our task would be impossible without our partners. He wrote recently in an EQUIP newsletter, "Without these alliances, our global mandate of training one million leaders around the world would be the slowest of endeavors and the blandest of journeys."[2]

In the same newsletter, Dr. Hull explained that Billy Hornsby, executive director of ARC, is a major proponent of partnerships. Here is a brief summary of Billy's arguments on behalf of partnerships or strategic alliances:

1. They force us out of isolation and require us to look at things from a different perspective.
2. They increase our influence.
3. They fuel our understanding.
4. They break logjams, shatter small thinking, and thrust us forward.
5. They enable us to leapfrog on the learning curve. We gain from lessons our partner has already learned on the road of experience.
6. They save time and resources, enabling both partners to accomplish more in kingdom work in a shorter time.

In summary, learn by example. Unleash the power of partnership! Then you, just like the ministry partners you've read about here, will *also* "accomplish more kingdom work in a shorter time." You will raise *more than money*!

8

Pastors and Partnership

Biblical stewardship is not God's way of raising money—it is God's way
of raising people into the likeness of His Son.

—Don Gray

William Carey is often referred to as "the father of modern missions."
But when he first shared his plans to go to India as a missionary, Carey
encountered much opposition. Only a small group of friends offered
any encouragement.

One day he sat down with his friends and held up before them a
rope. "*I* will go to India," he said, "if *you* will hold the rope." By "hold-
ing the rope" he meant praying for him consistently and supporting
him faithfully with their finances. His friends agreed and became partners in his ministry. He knew that even though only he would travel to
India, it was his partners who would make it possible. He understood
that, even in the background, they would share in the eternal rewards.

The concept of partnership is crucial in every God-ordained ministry, including the local church. Yet I find that parachurch leaders
tend to understand and embrace the concept more quickly than pastors. Perhaps this is because pastors far too frequently see partnership
as one-dimensional—primarily about giving of financial resources.

HIGH RISK AND HIGH POTENTIAL

Pastors must learn to see partnership in a much broader context. True partnership requires a pastor to

1. highly value each parishioner,
2. offer training and resources to help each individual become a devoted follower of Christ,
3. provide tools to help every person identify and cultivate his or her unique gifts and abilities,
4. find a ministry in which to use each congregant's gifts and abilities for kingdom impact, and
5. teach and model genuine biblical stewardship.

The pastor's platform preaching-teaching ministry can play a vital role in accomplishing these goals in the lives of many. But it is also essential for the pastor to invest time in insightful, focused, and personal instruction in the lives of a few individuals with unusually high potential. It is through these key leaders that the entire congregation can be discipled, trained, equipped, and mobilized to carry out the God-given mission of the local church.

Pastors are usually willing to help equip gifted laity for ministry and to play a key role in training those who demonstrate high leadership potential. Yet, because they fear being accused of "playing favorites," most pastors shy away from investing time with those to whom God has given the unusual ability to generate finances and make strategic kingdom investments. So, even when workers are equipped and leaders are developed, the local church limps along, struggling to cover operating expenses and never having funds for buildings and major equipment purchases. If the talented servant requires personal equipping, and the gifted potential leader is worthy of face-to-face training, doesn't the steward with major giving ability deserve a time and place to personally discuss biblical stewardship principles and be challenged about maximum giving for optimum kingdom impact?

But pastors often fail at this, so development representatives from parachurch ministries take the opportunity to fill up the vacuum left by pastors. No wonder parishioners often make their largest kingdom investments in ministries outside the local church. They invest in those who have taken the time to discuss biblical stewardship in depth with them and to educate and challenge them about investments in a vision that makes a significant difference for eternity.

Recently I encouraged a pastor to spend extra time with his wealthy parishioners to help them more fully understand biblical stewardship, to cast vision for the expanded ministry of the church, and to invite them to invest generously in a building project that is vital to that growing ministry. Obviously hesitant, the pastor asked, "How do I respond when I am criticized for giving too much time and attention to rich people in my congregation?" I explained that Jesus did not spend an equal amount of time with everyone either. I reminded him of the inordinate amount of time that Jesus invested in the Twelve, and then pointed out that He gave even more time individually to Peter, James, and John. He poured countless hours into these three, I asserted, because He saw extraordinary potential in them.

As our conversation continued, I asked the pastor some pointed questions: Would he feel free to invest additional time in the lives of people with special needs or those at high risk? Would he feel guilty spending an exorbitant amount of time with a parishioner who was suffering from a terminal illness? Would he mind being criticized for spending extra time with a teenager who is showing suicidal tendencies in the aftermath of his parents' divorce? All right, he agreed, there were "special needs" people in his care who may require a disproportionate amount of his time. At this point I stated quite emphatically that people of wealth in his congregation are also "special needs" people. They may, in fact, be the most spiritually "at-risk" individuals in his care. Why else would Jesus have said, "How hard it is for those who have riches to enter the kingdom of God" (Luke 18:24 NKJV)? He went on to say that "it is easier for a camel to go through the eye of a needle than for a rich man to enter the kingdom" (v. 25 NKJV).

I believe that the Proverbs writer recognized that men and women of wealth are special-needs people. Interestingly, he saw them in a high-risk category similar to those who are enslaved in poverty: "Give me neither poverty nor riches," he said, "but give me only my daily bread. Otherwise, I may have too much and disown you and say, 'Who is the LORD?' Or I may become poor and steal, and so dishonor the name of my God" (Prov. 30:8–9 NIV).

This wise writer also understood the incredible power of wealth. He knew that anyone with riches faces the temptation to develop a self-sufficient mind-set and thus think that he can live his life without daily depending on God. Isn't it interesting that we describe a highly successful person as "independently wealthy"? What a tragedy when this "independence" results in a failure to acknowledge God as the source of all treasures. When God is no longer seen as our source, He is no longer honored as the owner. Those who forget God's ownership will never adequately understand or practice stewardship.

Like a person lacking food, clothing, or shelter, a wealthy person is a special-needs individual who is at high risk in a different way. High risk and high potential combine to make the well-off individual a special target of the evil one. At the same time, because of the resources God has placed in the care of men and women of unusual wealth, they have the ability to make an extraordinary difference in a needy world. It is truly a spiritual ministry when a pastor invests extra time helping highly successful families understand biblical stewardship and discover the joy of giving generously and strategically for exponential kingdom results. What a blessing to help them "lay up treasures in heaven" as they increasingly reflect the giving nature of their Lord.

CHURCHWIDE GENEROSITY

While it is absolutely essential that the pastor find time to invest personally in parishioners with extraordinary giving potential, he or she must also help design and oversee an ongoing *churchwide* program to develop faithful, generous biblical stewards at *every level of income.* Stewardship education must be available to the whole congregation.

I believe the following steps by the pastor are basic to building a church filled with generous, joyful givers:

1. *Consistently and creatively communicate a compelling vision for the church's future.* Christian Community is a nonprofit research and program-development organization that focuses on the health of local churches and the communities they serve. Researchers at Christian Community have concluded, "People give to bold visions of what the church will become, to broadly held understandings of the mission of the church, and to people about whom they care. The same people who may look at a line item for Sunday school materials and feel it represents too much money will look at the picture of a child being served by the church and dig more deeply into their pockets."[1] People give to people and to God—not to line items in the budget.

2. *Model generosity.* Both the pastor and the church leadership need to give before asking others to give.

3. *Set aside at least one month each year to preach and teach about biblical stewardship.* While sermons should cover stewardship in a broad context (time, talents, etc.), at least one Sunday must be devoted specifically to the stewardship of financial resources. I recommend a "stewardship month" every six months. Several organizations offer excellent materials for use during a stewardship emphasis month. Author Stan Toler's integrated kit, The Cycle of Victorious Giving, contains everything you need, including model sermons, handouts, PowerPoint presentations, bulletin inserts, and more. It is available at www.stantoler.com. An e-manual titled *Guide to Increase Church Giving*, by Brian Kluth of Maximum Generosity (a biblical generosity resources and speaking ministry), shows church leaders how to successfully conduct what he calls an "all-church generosity initiative." You can order his manual at www.kluth.org/orderform.htm. Brian and Stan are experienced pastors who understand the pastor's role in developing biblical stewards. Their materials are superb.

4. *Realize that giving is about the condition of the* heart, *not the* *checking account.* Most of the dollars received by local churches are given by longtime-committed Christians. As such, I am convinced that high levels of giving are mainly motivated by high levels of commit-

---

The more Christlike your congregation becomes,
the more generous they will also become.

---

ment to Christ. Focus on helping believers become more like Jesus. The more Christlike your congregation becomes, the more generous they will also become, because stewardship is a lordship issue!

Christians who live under the lordship of Christ will exemplify His giving nature.

But not all parishioners are fully living under the lordship of Christ. They have not yet matured in their faith. We must not overlook new believers and others who attend faithfully but do not yet exemplify Christ's giving nature. Author Kennon L. Callahan writes:

> If you want to raise money, advance stewardship and deepen discipleship among long-time Christians, then you can focus on commitment and challenge. But when you want to advance giving, grow the stewardship and deepen the discipleship among the grassroots members, then be sure to focus on the motivations of compassion and community. Many people grow their stewardship out of a sense of compassion. Many grow their stewardship because of who we are as God's community. Stewardship is more than commitment, more than challenge: it is part of being a compassionate human being.[2]

He adds:

Grassroots members and unchurched people discover the Christian life through compassion and community. As we richly and fully share with them the spirit of compassion and the sense of community in our own spiritual growth and development, they will grow for-ward—at their own pace—to a deepening sense of commitment.[3]

5. *Be sure to communicate that giving is an act of faith and worship.* Always emphasize giving as an act of worship. Stewardship is a matter of trust—both my trusting God to provide His resources, and His trusting me to use those resources wisely and generously, for His honor and the building of His kingdom.

6. *Collect and share stories about generous givers who have experi-enced the joy of giving and the blessing of making an eternal difference.* Such stories can be found in books about well-known individuals who have modeled biblical stewardship. Perhaps even more effective are stories about unheralded people who have been unusually generous, often in spite of meager circumstances.

Also, on a regular basis, perhaps monthly, arrange for an individ-ual parishioner or family to share a brief (three minutes or less) per-sonal testimony, live or prerecorded, of what God has done through his or her giving and how that generosity has resulted in God's person-al blessings.

7. *Establish an annual operating budget, underwritten by weekly tithes and offerings.* Set up a separate budget for buildings and other major capital expenditures. This special capital budget provides a superb opportunity for Christians to be challenged to grow in their understanding and practice of generosity as biblical stewards. A major building project may require the church to partner with outside coun-sel to teach stewardship, develop leaders, and challenge biblical stew-ards to stretch to new levels of giving. For this purpose, I recommend Injoy Stewardship Services (www.injoystewardship.com).

In *Effective Church Finances*, Kennon L. Callahan argues for the establishment of what he calls a *mission budget*: "First, the mission budget is built on the major priorities of the congregation for the coming year. The congregation's long-range planning has developed these major priorities. Generally, effective congregations have no more than three to five major priorities at a time."[4]

Callahan emphasizes the importance of building the budget around the people to be served. He writes, "The mission budget is a people budget. People give money to people. A mission budget includes a focus on the people who will be helped through the congregation's major priorities. A mission budget also has a clear sense of the people who will be helping with each major priority, and the leaders who will advance the overall mission."[5] He adds:

> Describe the major priorities in terms of the specific key objectives that will be helpful in people's lives and destinies. Describe your major priorities as services we plan to share in mission. Let the spirit of your mission budget be: We plan to share these services with people in our congregation, in our community, in our country and across the world.[6]

People are not motivated to give to a budget of revenue and expenditures, income, and disbursements. They give generously to a church

---

Giving is not about "paying the bills,"
but about investing in the transformation of lives.

---

on a mission to meet real needs in the lives of real people. When the mission is clear and compelling, giving is not about "paying the bills," but about investing in the transformation of lives.

8. *Help worshipers understand the importance of estate and gift planning.* Offer estate planning seminars periodically to provide God's people with timely information about how to give through wills,

trusts, life insurance policies, and similar means. Such seminars can be very helpful to individuals who have the ability to give immediately from accumulated assets without damaging their financial health.

9. *Be sure that the children and youth are not overlooked in the stewardship education program.* It is crucial that every person in the congregation, regardless of age, understand the relationship between personal faith and the stewardship of one's God-given resources. Dick Towner, who serves with Willow Creek Association, was once asked what was the most satisfying aspect of being involved in helping churches teach stewardship. He replied:

> It is when church leaders realize that stewardship is a discipleship issue—not just helping a person get out of debt or giving more money to the church. Ben Patterson says there's no such thing as being right with God and being wrong with your money. That's very powerful and very true. It is well and good to help people get out of crushing consumer debt or to give generously, but it's so much deeper. Stewardship gets to the very core of helping a person become more Christ-like.[7]

STEWARDSHIP IS PARTNERSHIP

The little book of Haggai in the Old Testament has often spoken to me about the role of the biblical steward. The first chapter of the book finds the people of Israel recently returned from years in exile. Their homeland has become a vast wasteland. The temple, God's house, is a pile of rubble, but they have given no time or resources to rebuilding it. They are focused instead on trying to rebuild their own homes and barns. But God is not pleased with their neglect of the temple. Through the prophet, He confronts them about their misplaced priorities. He then instructs them to rebuild the temple, His dwelling place in the midst of His people, and reminds them of His special covenant with them.

So the people gather their limited resources and begin work on restoring God's house. Immediately the critics begin to lash out at them, trying to convince them that they are destined for failure. Let me paraphrase these outspoken negative people:

1. "The job is too big for you."
2. "Your resources are too small."
3. "Even if you finish the task, the temple will never compare with the glory of the former temple, built by Solomon, with his skilled craftsmen and vast wealth."

As the discouraged workers are about to abandon the job, God speaks words of comfort and encouragement through His prophet. Allow me also to paraphrase God's message to them:

1. "No job is too big for Me. Work, and I will work with you." God calls them to partnership.
2. "I am your source." God reminds them, "The silver is Mine, and the gold is Mine" (Hag. 2:8 NKJV). He calls them to trust Him and to channel His resources into the project He has assigned them.
3. "If you partner with Me, as colaborers and biblical stewards, I will 'fill this temple with glory'" (v. 7 NKJV). He assures them that whatever He fills with His presence is never inadequate or second-rate.

Yes, stewardship is partnership—partnership with the God of heaven in carrying out His mission here on planet Earth! What a wonderful privilege to have a key role in helping God's people discover the overflowing joy of partnering with the Lord Jesus as He builds His Church!

I believe strongly that people want their lives to count by having a part in a spiritual *movement*, not a *monument*. God's people are attracted by opportunities to make investments that change lives and destinies. They are not interested in giving to save an organization or an institution; they give to see souls saved!

Pastors, as I close this chapter, once again I quote author Kennon Callahan as he calls us to participate in the winning cause of God's mission on this planet:

> People are drawn to a winning cause. People are not drawn to groups that complain, lament, scold, and whine. Most of them already have enough of these negatives in their lives. People are drawn to groups that help them grow, develop, advance and build their lives.
>
> Those congregations having the confidence that they are participating in the winning cause of God's mission are the congregations that grow forward the generosity of their people. The more you describe your church as a winning cause, the more people you will reach and the more giving you will raise.
>
> People give to a winning cause, not a sinking ship. Share—with honesty and integrity—the ways in which you and your congregation are participating in a winning cause. We are the resurrection people. We are the Easter people. We are the people of hope.[8]

9

The Pitfalls of Partnership

God is looking for people through whom He can do the impossible—
what a pity that we plan only the things we can do by ourselves.

—A. W. Tozer

By now you understand the purpose and principles of partnership. You are no doubt firmly convinced of the power of partnership. But what about the *pitfalls* of partnership? *Pitfalls?* you may be saying. *But if I'm partnering with others, shouldn't it be easier?* Well . . . not necessarily. Why? Because obstacles can arise along *any* worthy journey. The ministry-partnership journey is no exception. Partnerships, after all, are made up of people, and people can be tempted to seek their *own* agendas. They can also be crippled by fear, limiting the success that could have been achieved by a strong, unified, visionary partnership. Whatever your venture, know that there will be hindrances along the way. Here are just a few to look out for.

Selfishness

Partnerships cannot operate on a one-way street. There must be a win-win relationship that helps all parties accomplish their God-given missions. The comedy duo of Abbott and Costello was so successful because each man not only understood his *own* role but also placed high value on the *other's* role. In fact, when the partnership was formed, Costello requested that all profits earned from the act be split 60/40 in favor of Abbott. "Comics are a dime a dozen," he explained. "Good straight men are hard to find."[1] This legendary comedic partnership prospered because neither partner was selfish. But a partnership fraught with selfishness is certain to fail.

INSECURITY

Partnerships cannot succeed if partners lack a clear understanding of the unique strengths they each contribute. Recognizing the value of their individual skill sets contributes to the success of the mission.

"Selfishness is the greatest curse of the human race."

—WILLIAM E. GLADSTONE,

19TH-CENTURY BRITISH STATESMAN

Partners feel *secure* employing their own strengths, rather than trying to imitate others. *Insecurity* breeds rigidity, egotism, jealousy, competition, and struggle for control.

For many years Dean Martin and Jerry Lewis were one of the most popular comedy twosomes in America, becoming the highest-paid comedic team in our nation. The pair made sixteen films together. When the act broke up in 1956, it made front-page news. Why did they go their separate ways? people wanted to know. Because each felt that he lived in the other's shadow. Neither was willing to share stardom with the other. Insecurity ended one of the most successful comedic teams ever. [2]

LACK OF COMMUNICATION

When partners fail to communicate honestly and frequently, the potential for misunderstanding rapidly grows. Even though a ministry

partner may be thousands of miles away, perhaps even on the opposite side of the globe, it is never distance that separates us—it is always
lack of communication. Partnerships are frequently more difficult to
maintain than to start. And failure to communicate is the chief reason
for problems.

A recent corporate scandal involved WorldCom, the telecommuni-
cations giant presided over by Bernie Ebbers. Ebbers's key associate
was his chief financial officer, Scott Sullivan. These two men were very
different in their personal lives. Ebbers typically dressed in jeans and
cowboy boots. He was swaggering and bold. Sullivan, in contrast, was
a strait-laced financial whiz kid who favored blue shirts and ties.
Together they built a powerful company that amazed Wall Street.

Ebbers once publicly praised Sullivan for the company's success,
saying, "All the credit goes to him." But privately the relationship was
difficult. The men bore resentments toward each other that occasionally bubbled to the surface. When the company began to suffer difficulties, there were times when the two executives barely spoke to each
other.

When Ebbers went on trial in federal court in Manhattan, Sullivan
was the chief witness against his former boss.[3] The case is a strong
warning of how partners who once valued and needed each other can
become adversaries. Lack of honest and regular communication is
usually the culprit. Keep the lines of communication open.

Egos and Logos

Sometimes partnership requires us to minister where we will not
receive the recognition we think we deserve. EQUIP is currently
involved in partnerships with several organizations that work with the
persecuted church in "closed" countries. Circumstances in some of
these nations require that our name and logo be omitted from all of
the workbooks and other resources used in those countries. Further,
security issues, including the safety of our ministry partners, prevent
us from providing specific information to our constituents about the

impact of our ministry there. Imagine what could happen if we allowed our egos to get in the way, demanding the credit for our ministerial influence and teaching materials.

An interesting partnership in the Old Testament involved Saul and Samuel. Though Samuel had been the leader in Israel for years, he

---

"It is amazing what can be done
if no one cares who gets the credit."

—MARK TWAIN

---

willingly laid aside his status to publicly honor Saul. Samuel was not envious of the new king. He understood his role as a prophet and didn't need a royal position to carry out his responsibilities. He refused to become a victim of his own ego.

A SCARCITY MIND-SET

Every segment of society has begun to see the benefits of partnerships. Ministry leaders, business leaders, educators, government officials, technology experts, medical researchers—choose any field and you will find leaders forging new partnerships. Partnerships pool resources and people, producing creative solutions for the benefit of the whole.

But people who have never experienced the power of partnerships can mistakenly believe that there's "not enough to go around." If they share with others, they reason, they will lose something. Consequently, they strive to hoard everything for themselves. Trying to partner in ministry with such a person is difficult. If you do succeed, forming additional partnerships will be even more difficult. You may find that your partner bucks your every suggestion or endeavor, because he or she has fallen prey to a *scarcity mind-set*. This attitude *opposes* partnerships.

Those who value ministry partnership live with an *abundance mind-set*. They see God as the provider, always confident that He has unlimited resources. Generosity becomes a core value. "Abundance thinkers" understand that when they share with others, they always receive back more than they give.

These are just a few of the dangers you may face as you seek to form lasting and profitable ministry partnerships, but if you can leap the hurdles, the benefits far outweigh the difficulties. Listen to what one of our partners wrote, just one example of what we receive regularly from our ministry partners: "Our partnership with EQUIP has already yielded visible fruit as large numbers of men and women have stepped up to the challenge of leading the church in their area of the world. The leadership training these developing leaders are receiving through our partnership with you is doubtlessly making a powerful eternal impact."[4]

Ministry partnerships are powerful. I believe they please the heart of God and invite His favor and blessing. The Great Commission mandate before us is huge. Some say the task is impossible. But our God is a God of the impossible. He can help us hurdle every hindrance, break down every barrier, and overcome every obstacle. And together we can reach our world for Christ!

Part III

Relational Funding: Accomplishing God's Dreams Through Relationships

In October 1963, my wife, Winnie, and I were appointed to serve as missionaries to Native Americans in the Southwest. Because we were serving with an interdenominational "faith" mission agency, we had to raise our own financial support. On February 1, 1964, I resigned from my position with a growing business in my hometown and hit the road to "raise money."

My first speaking engagement was at a church in the South. The weekend began with a delicious meal in the home of my host family on Saturday evening. After dinner, we talked for more than two hours. I listened as the dad, mom, and their two children each shared personal testimonies of their spiritual journeys. Then I explained my own faith journey and how God had laid a special burden on my heart to see Native Americans won to Christ. Our hosts asked many questions about Winnie and me and our God-given dream to reach the "forgotten Americans" with the gospel. We laughed together, and we also shed some tears as I shared about the spiritual and physical needs of American Indians. I also described how the Lord was opening doors for us to make an eternal difference in their lives.

Our conversation continued late into the evening. As their dog climbed into my lap, the mother asked, "How can we help you reach Native Americans for Christ?" (I can still remember answering her while patting the dog with one hand and juggling a dish of ice cream with the other!) In reply, I underscored the importance of faithful prayer support and presented to the family the opportunity to partner with us financially. I then expressly asked them to join our support team. The father told me that they would pray about their level of partnership and then suggested that we have a time of prayer before going to bed.

The next morning, I talked for about twenty minutes to a Sunday school class full of teenagers. That was followed by worship in the sanctuary, where I delivered the message to about two hundred people. I began by sharing my testimony and our calling to minister to American Indians. At the end of the message, I asked for prayer support and financial partnerships.

Afterward, as I stood at the back of the church with the pastor, many people greeted me warmly and promised to remember Winnie and me in prayer. But only one person, an elderly lady, responded with a gift to our ministry. She handed me twenty dollars.

After lunch with my host family, as I prepared to leave for another church, where I would speak that evening, the father asked to spend a few minutes with me before I departed. As we stepped into the living room, he embraced me and, with tears flowing, expressed his gratitude to God for bringing me to their home. He handed me a very generous check, and on the commitment card he indicated his family's intentions to give liberally each month. As we talked for another half hour or so, I realized that we had become friends. In that brief time we had established a *relationship* based on mutual respect and trust. Together, we initiated a ministry partnership that linked his passion to be an effective biblical steward with my passion to win souls to the Savior.

As I drove to my next speaking engagement, I realized that "raising money" was not my real mission. Yes, I needed to build a strong and loyal support team, but I was beginning to understand that it would not be built from the platform.

I have learned many more lessons about establishing and maintaining friendships with those from all walks of life—from friends with modest incomes to the very wealthy, from college students to retirees, and from pastors to executives. But the lessons I learned that February weekend in 1964 changed the course of my life. I started on a new journey that has continued all of these years—a very special journey that has led me to establish long-lasting friendships based on integrity and Christian love, to endeavor to add value to the lives of ministry partners, and to ask friends to become generously and faithfully involved with ministries that are producing maximum impact for the kingdom of God.

Since those early days, I have been a missionary, president of a Christian college, and an executive for a major missions agency. Currently, it is my privilege to serve as the senior vice president for EQUIP. In all of these places of kingdom service, I have had the joy of helping Christian men and women strategically invest millions of dollars in Great Commission work. But "raising money" has never been the objective. My passion has been to minister to God's people by helping them experience the fulfillment of practicing biblical stewardship. After all, development work done God's way isn't about raising money. It is about helping people understand that as faithful stewards, we are reflecting the giving nature of Christ.

WE NEED EACH OTHER

There is no such thing as a "self-made" man. We are made up of thousands of others. Everyone who has ever done a kind deed for us, or spoken one word of encouragement to us, has entered into the make-up of our character and of our thoughts, as well as our success.

—George Burton Adams, 19th-century author

Years ago, Bible scholars met together at a summit in an attempt to distill the Christian faith into a single, defining phrase. But at the end of the summit, they were actually able to summarize our faith in a single *word*. Based on the Scriptures, they concluded, that one word was *relationships*.[1]

Not only is faith about relationships, but our *lives* are all about relationships. Our successes and failures are inextricably linked to how we handle them. In fact, when you extract all of the unnecessary things about life, all that remains is relationships. The most important relationship we have is a vertical one—with our heavenly Father. But the Word of God also instructs us to pursue horizontal relationships—with two different sectors of people. We are to connect relationally

---

When you extract all of the unnecessary things about life, all that remains is relationships.

---

with (1) those who need to be introduced to our Savior, and (2) our fellow believers in the body of Christ.

Interestingly, Corporate America is now taking a second look at the impact of relationships on company success. Peter Drucker has been writing for half a century in terms of businesses as *social* communities. But now others are joining his quest to replace the outdated management style where people are viewed as machines, not human beings. Historically, the quantity of their employees' production was all that mattered to management. Today, more and more business leaders see the value of *human-centered management.* Keith Ferrazzi, currently known as "the ultimate networker" in the business sector, states in his book *Never Eat Alone,* "The secret is in reaching out to other people. What distinguishes highly successful people from everyone else is the way they use the power of relationships—so that everyone wins."[2]

Margaret Wheatley is a consultant, speaker, and best-selling author in the business world. "Relationships are all there is," she writes. "Everything in the universe only exists because it is in relationship to everything else. Nothing exists in isolation. We have to stop pretending we are individuals that can go it alone."[3] Isn't it fascinating that the corporate world is becoming a proponent of biblical principles, and they don't even know it?

Another segment of our population, the medical community, affirms the importance of relationships to one's health. Twenty years ago, Leonard Syme, a professor of epidemiology at the University of California at Berkeley, alleged that people's social ties and support systems are good preventive medicine for both physical ailments and mental-emotional-behavior problems.[4] In his studies on mortality and disease rates, he discovered that Japan was number one in the world with respect to health. He concluded that the reason for their overall good health is their close social, cultural, and traditional ties. The more positive relationships people have, he decided, the better the health and the lower the death rate. Conversely, the more isolated people are, the poorer the health and the higher the death rate. Bottom line? *We need each other.* We can only live in relationships.

Emperor Frederick II, who ruled the Holy Roman Empire in the thirteenth century, once carried out a rather crude and cruel experiment. He wanted to know what man's original language was—Hebrew, Greek, or Latin. He decided to isolate a few infants from the sound of the human voice. He reasoned that they would eventually speak the natural tongue of man. Wet nurses were sworn to absolute silence, and though it was difficult for them, they abided by the rule. The babies never heard a word—not a sound from a human voice. Within several months they all died.[5]

God, our Creator, never intended for us to go it alone. The significance of relationships in God's economy is verified throughout Scripture. As you search through God's Word, you will find the concept of loving and caring for "one another" in verse after verse. And the best way to do this is to fulfill the Great Commission: spread the gospel around the planet and accomplish God's dreams.

In Part III, we will discover how we can use *relationships* to accomplish God's dreams through *relational funding*—building relationships with people, who will invest in birthing and building relationships with God.

10

Relational Funding: An Overview

In a great trial of affliction the abundance of their joy and their deep poverty abounded in the riches of their liberality . . . According to their ability, yes, and beyond their ability, they were freely willing, imploring us with much urgency that we would receive the gift and the fellowship of the ministering to the saints . . . They first gave themselves to the Lord, and then to us.

—Paul the Apostle,
of the churches of Macedonia, 2 Corinthians 8:1–5 NKJV

A Matter of the Heart

Relational funding is rooted in the idea that relationships with givers should be established around the desire to advance their spiritual growth. "It is a vision of fundraising as a process that is as much concerned with the effect on people's character and values as with the effect on organizations' incomes."[1]

In recent years, I have had the joy of getting to know Daryl Heald, president of Generous Giving, Inc., in Chattanooga, Tennessee. Daryl believes that development officers all too often see their work in terms of *tactics* and *transactions*. The real focus, he says, must be on *heart transformation*. In the quarterly newsletter of the Evangelical Council on Financial Accountability (ECFA), Daryl wrote:

When we think through our giving transformationally, we ask only one question: Why? Why give in the first place? Why not keep more for myself? Why does God need it? Why has He asked me to participate? This line of questioning moves us into the theological and philosophical realm—our hearts.

For too long, givers and ministries have focused exclusively on tactics and transactions, underestimating the need for transformation. We have unwittingly created and perpetuated a culture of frugal tipping, rather than generous giving.[2]

It is easy for giving to become nothing more than a mathematical formula or a legalistic duty. In his book *Field of Gold*, Andy Stanley counters that "giving should be a relational experience. If you don't feel closer to God," he says, "as if He's compelling you to give and your gifts are an expression of your heartfelt devotion back to Him—then you may be missing the whole point of giving."[3]

In light of this, the role of the development representative should be about *raising more than money*. It must be about raising the level of every giver's devotion to God.

To do this, the representative must:

- build relationships
- cast vision
- teach biblical stewardship
- ask personally for a commitment
- thank givers consistently
- report honestly and faithfully

Yes, it is a process, but it is so much more! It is a true *spiritual ministry*! What a blessed privilege to help God's people discover the joy of living not only in an intimate relationship but also a financial partnership with our heavenly Father. When givers' hearts are fully attuned to God's heart and His priorities, giving becomes an exciting act of worship.

A Biblical Example

Years ago I heard development consultant and conference speaker Bob Fraley say, "The Bible is the greatest manual ever written on development." I agree. In fact, in *Growing Givers' Hearts*, Thomas Jeavons and Rebekah Basinger identify the apostle Paul as a master of develop-

---

When givers' hearts are fully attuned to God's heart and His priorities, giving becomes an exciting act of worship.

---

ment: "Paul sets forth the ideals around which Christian fundraising should be organized in emphasizing that giving should be an act of joy, an expression of one's own experience of and trust in God's love and care, and a reflection of one's sense of being a partner in God's work in the world."[4]

Let's look at some of the ways Paul modeled relational funding as he sought assistance for the saints:

1. He asked for financial partnership from those with whom he had *first* built a relationship (2 Cor. 9:1–4).
2. He understood the importance of a personal visit (2 Cor. 9:5).
3. He promised a face-to-face visit (1 Cor. 16:2–3, 5; 11:34).
4. He emphasized proportionate giving (1 Cor. 16:2).
5. He recognized the need to ask (2 Cor. 8:10–11).
6. He made a personal appeal (1 Cor. 16:1).
7. He asked givers to give generously (2 Cor. 9:6, 11).
8. He insisted upon accountability and the highest ethical standards (2 Cor. 8:18–22).

What made Paul so effective at raising the funds to meet a specific need? First, Paul understood that God uses *people* to provide for His work. Because Paul prayed for the guidance of the Holy Spirit and established friendships with many people, he could easily identify potential financial partners. And once he found them, Paul did not simply *hint* about a need; he asked them *personally* to give.

Paul also succeeded because he realized that giving is emotional. He did not ignore people's feelings and responses. Instead, he challenged, commended, encouraged, and thanked them. He boasted about them to others. He even went so far as to compare their giving with others'.

An Organizational Example

Guiding Principles of EQUIP

It has been my pleasure to be involved in the development activities of EQUIP since its beginning in 1996. To succeed at relational funding, EQUIP employs the following guiding principles, setting a very high standard for the EQUIP team.

1. We believe that God is the source of all financial resources that are given to our ministry.
2. We believe that development done God's way focuses on the spiritual maturation of givers, and that every development activity must be saturated with prayer.
3. We believe that connecting with people in the most personal way possible is crucial to effective ministry and successful development.
4. We believe that the giver is always more important than the gift. Our donors are our friends and ministry partners; they are not "revenue sources"!
5. We believe it is biblical to ask Christian people to give generous and strategic gifts that will produce maximum results for God's Kingdom.
6. We believe that we are accountable to God and His people to use the funds they provide as wisely and effectively as we know how. We believe givers should be promptly thanked and kept well informed of the progress of the work in which they have invested.

7. We believe that all written and verbal presentations, including descriptions of financial needs, must be current, complete, and accurate. There must be no exaggeration of facts or any other misleading communication. "Not that I am looking for a gift, but I am looking for what may be credited to your account" (Phil. 4:17 NIV). *How* we think is crucial in building strong and lasting relationships with our ministry partners. *What* we think will control our actions.

WRONG THINKING:

1. Thinking that an organization or ministry will attract support just because it is a wonderful cause.
2. Thinking that sending printed materials exclusively will build strong and lasting relationships with givers. (Send people to connect with people.)
3. Thinking that an organization has needs. (People, not organizations, have needs.)
4. Thinking that everyone should give the same amount.
5. Thinking that people will be offended if they are asked to give.
6. Thinking that all large gifts come from wealthy people.
7. Thinking that raising money is the priority. (Building relationships is the priority.)

WRONG ACTIONS:

1. Failing to see relational funding in development as a spiritual ministry to givers.
2. Failing to pray.
3. Failing to connect with people by listening, serving, and adding value to their lives.

4. Failing to clearly communicate a vision and strategy to meet real needs in the lives of real people.
5. Failing to explain how your friends can partner with you to make a significant difference.
6. Failing to ask personally (face-to-face).
7. Failing to ask for a specific amount based on the donor's capacity to give, interests, relationship, and motivation.
8. Failing to communicate a sense of urgency.
9. Failing to follow up . . . stopping too soon in the relationship.
10. Failing to regularly thank and report to ministry partners.

As we said at the beginning of this chapter, development is *spiritual ministry*. The *focus* is on the giver's *heart* as the Christian development officer teaches and models biblical stewardship. Biblical relational funding, therefore, has a three-part goal: to motivate believers

1. to mature in their faith as they obediently practice stewardship;
2. to discover the joy of giving as an act of worship, prompted by the Holy Spirit; and
3. to invest strategically and generously in Great Commission work.

I have discovered that four "*L* words" are crucial steps in building strong and lasting relationships with ministry partners. These verbs require deliberate action on the part of ministries and development representatives. Each *L* word is also an acronym that further explains the active verb. The ministry partner (donor) is the direct object of each verb. See Figure 10.1.

In the chapters ahead, we will examine each of these vital processes as we learn to make relational funding effective for your ministry as you faithfully endeavor to accomplish God's dreams.

L.O.V.E Them   **L.E.A.D Them**   **L.I.N.K. Them**   **L.I.F.T Them**

Love Lead Link Lift

Process	Key Focus/Key Value	Result
Listen to them Open your heart to them Value them Exemplify generosity	**Communication** based on: *Trust*	**Friendship**
Lay out the dream Explain the strategy Ask them for partnership Deliver what you promise	**Connection** based on: *Vision*	**Relationship**
Lift them up in prayer Involve them Never take them for granted Keep them informed	**Ministry** based on: *Partnership*	**Multiplied Results**
Listen to them Invest in them Facilitate their dreams Thank them often	**Lifestyle** based on: *Stewardship*	**Legacy**

Figure 10.1—EQUIP's Relational Funding Model

11

A Closer Look at L.O.V.E. Them

And now abide faith, hope, love, these three; but the greatest of these is love.

—Paul the Apostle, 1 Corinthians 13:13 NKJV

In Chapter 10 I introduced four indispensable steps to forging strong, long-term relationships with ministry partners. In this chapter, we will begin to look at the relational funding process one step at a time. In figure 10.1 you saw that there are four phases of the process, each containing four steps. As the development representative builds relationships with givers and potential givers, he or she will repeat the process countless times with each person. Furthermore, moving from one phase to the next in the relationship, the representative does not abandon any previous phase. In other words, when the relationship is fully built, all four phases are engaged.

L.O.V.E. THEM

Listen to them.
Open your heart to them.
Value them.
Exemplify generosity.

The first phase is *L.O.V.E. them*. It has everything to do with the atti-tude of development representatives—about how they view their work and about their feelings toward the people they serve. Phase I emphasizes that development work is ministry, overflowing from the heart of one who truly cares about others. It is the beginning point of building authentic, long-lasting relationships with donors and poten-tial donors. In discussing the complexities of development work, author John Frank boldly concludes that, really, development is *sim-ple*. He said in his book, *The Ministry of Development*, "It is people helping people."[1]

Timothy Smith, in his book, *Donors Are People Too*, explains that a development representative initiates a relationship with this question in mind: Is there a way I can minister to this person? He adds, "I want to know if there's a way I can invest, be helpful, pray, love. It's possible the person may give to my organization eventually, but that will be a by-product, not the end-product, of the relationship."[2]

When I meet with givers or prospective givers, I do my very best to focus on them, not on me or the organization I represent. While build-ing a relationship based on a shared vision to make a real, eternal differ-ence, a friendship results. As we laugh together, cry together, pray to-gether, share burdens, and celebrate victories, we forge an ever deeper and richer relationship. As I faithfully endeavor to minister to each giver, the level of trust grows. Timothy Smith sums it up this way:

> My goal in major donor ministry is to grow friends, to minister truly and deeply to individuals, whether they ever give again or not. We become stakeholders in each other's lives. But because of my passion for my organization's mission, and because of the deepening relationship between that donor and me, it's almost inevitable that the donor will grow more committed to the min-istry I'm involved with. His giving, then, will be a by-product of that commitment. And at the end of the day, I will lay my head on my pillow with a deep sense of satisfaction, not just because

someone contributed to my ministry, but because I contributed. I didn't just represent a ministry: I *did* ministry.[3]

L – LISTEN TO THEM

This may well be the most vital part of the relationship-building process. No strong friendship can be built without open and honest communication. Hence, it is my firm opinion that in the initial phase of the process, the development representative must spend at least 70 percent of his time listening. This requires discipline and focus, because we who are involved in development work like to talk! We are

---

> *"Effective listeners remember that 'words have no meaning—people have meaning' . . . We often misinterpret each other's messages while under the illusion that a common understanding has been achieved."*
>
> —LARRY BARKER

---

in the "telling business": we love to tell others about our organization and the impact it is having. But until we have listened to a giver or prospective giver, we cannot possibly minister to that person, and certainly we cannot know his or her dreams, values, and priorities. If we don't know a person's dreams in life, how can we ever connect those dreams with our dreams in a mutual commitment or partnership that truly makes a difference?

William Sturtevant, in his book *The Artful Journey*, asserts that the first important characteristic of an outstanding fund-raiser is impeccable character. "The second most important characteristic," he then declares, "fortunately one that can be learned, is effective listening.

There just isn't a substitute. The goal of the effective listener is to encourage the prospect to talk, then listen in order to understand his or her views, unique needs, and fears relating to the giving decision. To be effective requires that you listen without an agenda. It is in this manner that you can truly become a partner and consultant to your prospect as he or she works through the gift decision."[4] Finally, he employs the term *active listening*, describing this necessary skill as "proactive. It involves the use of questions to elicit and clarify information."[5]

Design your questions to offer potential contributors the opportunity to talk freely about themselves, their families, their vocations, their hobbies, and their dreams. As you listen, you begin to learn what is important to them. You can immediately begin to show interest in the things they value. Many times, we talk too much because we want to be interest*ing*. But in building relationships, isn't it more important to be interest*ed* in people and *their* interests? Mark Sanborn, in his book *The Fred Factor*, says, "It may be true that *interesting* people attract attention, but I believe *interested* people attract appreciation."[6]

I recall meeting several years ago with the owner of a very successful business. Because he had only agreed to give me fifteen minutes of his time, I felt pressured to spend most of the time talking about the ministry I represented. I must confess that I dominated the conversation. Later, as I walked toward my car, reflecting on the meeting, it was almost heartbreaking for me to have to admit that little or no relationship building had taken place. I had not even started the journey toward a lasting friendship. I knew little more about this proprietor than when I entered his office. I promised myself right then that if he ever again agreed to see me, the meeting would be radically different.

Several months later he somewhat reluctantly agreed to a short, ten-minute meeting. This time I began by asking a question about his family. Soon he was telling me about his love for his wife and his daily prayer that she would give her life to Christ. We stopped our conversation and prayed together for her salvation. When I asked him about his hobbies, he began to tell me about a NASCAR race he had attended the previous Saturday evening. I am interested in racing too! For almost an hour we swapped NASCAR stories, talking about our favorite drivers and discussing the most exciting races we had ever watched.

Finally, when I suggested that I should probably be going, he said, "Let me ask my assistant to delay my next appointment. I want you to tell me about your ministry and how I can help." A friendship formed that day that remained strong until his death. His giving to our organization increased every year of his life, and he left a sizable gift through his estate. And all because I had finally learned the value of "active listening."

Active listening must include the following measures:

1. Concentrate on what is being said.
2. Ask questions that show real interest in the speaker.
3. Give the speaker plenty of time to answer, and do not interrupt.
4. Offer affirming feedback.
5. Maintain eye contact.
6. Make mental notes of what the speaker is saying.
7. Be sure your body language indicates real interest—leaning forward, nodding your head, smiling, etc.
8. Avoid any body movements or actions that indicate lack of interest, such as looking away, daydreaming, slumping, tapping your fingers on table, etc.
9. Offer to pray with the person if any special needs are mentioned.
10. After the meeting, make written notes of key points and other information that will form the basis of future conversations.

It has been my privilege to know Dr. John C. Maxwell for more than thirty years. Over the past decade I have traveled with John to over 150 conferences in the United States and have journeyed with him to Asia, Africa, Europe, and Latin America. I know John to be a very good listener. But in the book he coauthored with Les Parrott, *25 Ways to Win with People*, John admits that he has not *always* been a good listener. In this book, he shares the ideas that helped him become a good listener. First, he admonished readers, you must "listen to understand." "The fundamental cause of nearly all communication problems," he wrote, "is that people don't listen to understand; they listen to reply."[7] John then quotes David Burns, a medical doctor and professor of psychiatry at the University of Pennsylvania: "The biggest mistake you can make in trying to talk convincingly is to put your highest priority on expressing your ideas and feelings. What most people really want is to be listened to, respected, and understood. The moment people see that they are being understood, they become more motivated to understand your point of view."[8] John adds, "Listening with the heart produces a win-win situation in relationships."[9]

So does listening to what's *not* being said. In fact, John Maxwell quotes Peter Drucker as saying, "The most important thing in communication is to hear what isn't being said."[10]

My dad passed away on Christmas Eve morning when I was only eleven. The years immediately following his death were extremely difficult for me. I began to believe that no one cared about me, not even God.

One summer, when I was thirteen, I attended a church camp. The Bible teacher, a very distinguished professor, was an expert in Hebrew. I was captivated by his knowledge of the Old Testament. After an especially challenging lesson about Joseph and his sufferings, I wanted desperately to talk with the speaker and to share the hurt I was feeling. But I was much too shy. And besides, I thought, why would this important man want to talk with just a kid?

The next day, as the teacher was walking across the campgrounds, he noticed me sitting on a bench under a shade tree. "Young man," he said to me, "how are you today?" Though I tried to act as if everything was fine, he must have detected a problem when I replied, "Doing pretty good." He immediately came over and sat beside me on the bench, and I talked. I am convinced today that he was listening with his heart and heard not only what I was saying with words, but what I was *not* saying.

For more than an hour the professor gave "just a kid" his undivided attention. He made me feel as if I was the most important person in the whole universe. He kept his eyes on me and never let anything distract

---

"Sometimes the most revealing part of a message isn't found in the words themselves but in the subtle messages wrapped around those words. Failure to pick up on these 'secret messages' may leave you blind to what is really being communicated."

—DIANNA BOOHER, COMMUNICATIONS EXPERT

---

him. Nearby, dozens of teenagers were playing ball, yelling loudly, and having loads of fun, but never once did he look away from me. He listened with empathetic eyes as I bared my heart and soul.

After sharing stories of how God helped him overcome hurts in his own life, he placed his arm around me and lifted me in prayer. A special friendship was formed that day that has spanned more than fifty years. This godly gentleman, Dr. Dennis Kinlaw, is now well into his eighties, but he remains one of my heroes. He is one of the people who have most significantly influenced my life and ministry.

O – OPEN YOUR HEART TO THEM

When I became the president of a Christian college in 1980, I explained to the student body my "open door, open office, open home, open heart" policy. I wanted them to know that I cared deeply about each of them and would be available to listen to their problems. Students did not need an appointment to see me. Unless I was in a meeting of dire importance, I would stop whatever I was doing to welcome a student into my office. And while I don't remember the hundreds of conversations across the nine years that I led the college, I do recall many with students who arrived at my office or home discouraged and on the verge of quitting college. Dozens were ready to abandon God's call on their lives to ministry. As I listened to their concerns and opened my heart to them by sharing my own personal and spiritual journey, including the difficult and painful early years, we began to connect at the heart level. We established trust. Students began to honestly reveal the deep needs in their lives. Our prayer times together were life-changing as the Holy Spirit brought new strength and determination to struggling young followers of Christ. Today, scores of these young men and women serve Christ around the world as pastors, teachers, and missionaries.

I believe the key to an open heart is *authenticity*. Mark Sanborn writes:

> Be real. This is the direct opposite of the prevailing wisdom in our culture today, which is "fake it until you make it." The intent is to become who you want to be by acting as if you are already that person. The only problem with that strategy is that you're a fake! The prerequisite for relationship building is trust. At its most basic level, trust is built on believing that people are who they represent themselves to be.[11]

Opening your heart by honestly sharing your personal faith journey reveals who you really are and why you do what you do. It explains why you are so passionate about your ministry. I believe when a person of integrity, with a caring heart, representing an organization that is making an eternal difference, builds a relationship with an individual who cares, amazing and wonderful things will happen!

But open-hearted people have to be more than honest; they must also be *available* and *responsive*. I give my cell phone number to all of our major donors. They know that they can call me day or night, even on weekends. When I cannot answer the phone personally and callers must leave messages, returning those calls as quickly as possible is a high priority for me. Recently, while I was in Beijing, I received a

---

"Be who you are and say what you feel because those who mind don't matter and those who matter don't mind."

—Dr. Seuss (1904–1991)

---

phone call at 2:00 a.m., with an urgent prayer request from a donor on the opposite side of the globe. After listening to the need of my dear friend, we closed our conversation with a time of prayer. A few days later, as my plane taxied to the gate in Atlanta, I called this friend to get an update on his situation. It was my second cell phone call upon my return to the States (the first was to my wife!).

V – Value Them

Development representatives must place a high value on people. We must see every person as God's unique creation, with the potential to make a difference. And though stewardship of our time and the organization's resources requires that we invest strategically in those with the greatest potential, we highly value every giver.

In dozens of conferences through the years, I have heard John Maxwell talk about the importance of "adding value to people." He is passionate about this. He said to me recently, "Doug, my greatest joy in ministry is to invest in others, to feel that I am truly adding value to their lives." Many times I have heard John explain to conference attendees the ways to effectively do this. With his permission, I list them here:

We add value to people when we . . .

- value people
- make ourselves more valuable
- know and relate to what they value
- value what God values

In my travels with John, I have seen him in conversations with hundreds of people from countless cultures and backgrounds. I have watched him interact with the poorest of the poor to heads of state (presidents and prime ministers), but never once have I heard him talk down to anyone. He always listens intently, affirms others, expresses thanks, and looks for ways to invest in them. John values people because he knows that God values them—enough to send His Son to die for their sins.

To add value to people, we must have something to offer them. After all, we can't give what we don't have. The development officer who truly desires to add value to others must daily grow spiritually and professionally. In *25 Ways to Win with People,* John writes:

> When you acquire knowledge, learn a new skill, or gain experience, you not only improve yourself, but you also increase your ability to help others. In 1974 I committed myself to the pursuit of personal growth. I knew that it would help me to be a better minister, so I began to continually read books, listen to tapes, attend conferences, and learn from better leaders. At this time, I had no idea that this commitment would be the most important thing I would ever do to help others. But that has turned out to be the case. As I improve myself, I am better able to help others improve. The more I grow, the more I can help others grow. The same will be true for you. If you want to add value to people, you must make yourself more valuable.[12]

Because John and Larry Maxwell knew my passion for the Great Commission and the overflowing joy I find in helping God's people make strategic investments in reaching the nations for Christ, I was asked to be the first employee of EQUIP when it was launched in 1996. John and Larry's belief in me has opened doors for me to minister in America and in dozens of nations on every continent. I could never have opened those doors alone.

In the ministry of development, we understand the importance of achieving results, but we also understand that *how* we treat people is even more significant. The most valuable development principle I ever learned is this: the giver is always more important than the gift.

E – EXEMPLIFY GENEROSITY

Development representatives often feel that their most important role is to challenge others to become generous givers. Frankly, I think they have to first *be* generous givers. They must embody generosity before they can effectively lead others on the journey to experiencing the joy of giving. Good leaders must be out front, showing the way.

Generosity, for the Christian giver, begins in the heart. It takes root inside of those who have experienced God's own generous love. Then, with our hearts full of His love, we pour generosity upon others. Why? Because God's love moves us to action. "The love of Christ compels us," says Paul the Apostle (2 Cor. 5:14 NKJV). Self-centeredness is *de*throned in our lives, and Jesus is *en*throned! Since our passion is to be like Him, our giving is unselfish. It is not motivated by a desire for publicity, photo ops, and ways to enhance our image. We want to become more like our Lord, the greatest giver of all. "We all, . . . beholding as in a mirror the glory of the Lord, are being transformed into the same image from glory to glory" (2 Cor. 3:18 NKJV). Giving is an outgrowth of our relationship with Jesus Christ, and generosity becomes a lifestyle. Our stewardship of time, talents, and resources is at the very core of who we are. Only then can we say with Paul, "Imitate me, just as I also imitate Christ" (1 Cor. 11:1 NKJV).

Stan Toler is one of the most generous people I have ever known. If we could examine his spiritual DNA, we would find generosity in every fiber of his being. I first met Stan when he was nineteen and working a part-time job. He was struggling to make ends meet, paying his way through college in preparation to become a pastor.

One night, Stan attended a missionary service where Winnie and I were speaking. As we presented our need for prayer and financial partners in our ministry to Native Americans, he signed a commitment card indicating his plan to give monthly to our personal support. For more than thirty-five years now, Stan has invested faithfully in our ministry.

In his book *God Has Never Failed Me, but He Sure Has Scared Me to Death a Few Times*, Stan describes one of the occasions when he felt God telling him that he should send a special gift to my family:

> Moving to Tampa, Florida to become a young church planter with my new bride, Linda, was indeed an exercise in faith. We drove our car from our college campus in Ohio to Florida by faith. And eating lots of Hamburger Helper became a way of life! We simply learned to rely on the grace of God to meet our every need.
>
> I remember on one occasion, I felt led of the Lord to send $50 to the Carters, missionaries to the American Indians in Arizona, even though I wasn't sure why I was supposed to. Linda and I examined our checkbook and found just $54! We sent the $50 anyway and the next day, I went back to the post office. To my surprise, my college roommate, J. Michael Walters, had sent us a letter and enclosed a love gift of $50! (Pretty amazing, considering that he was a student at Asbury Seminary.)
>
> Obviously, we were satisfied because God had met our need overnight! But the Carters wrote back two weeks later and said, "Your check for $50 arrived just on time. We were preparing to cancel a doctor's appointment for our daughter, Angie, because we didn't have the money." Would you believe, they needed exactly $50![13]

When Winnie and I relocated to the Atlanta area in 1997, we moved into a newly built home. I soon discovered that countless projects needed to be done for the house to be made livable—and I am *very* "handyman challenged." A large discount store nearby offered tools and supplies, but every time I went seeking advice, either I could not locate a salesperson or the one I found knew absolutely nothing that would help me. Frustrated, I would head toward home—without tools or materials.

One day, on my way back home, I saw a small hardware store, where I decided to stop. When I stepped inside, it looked like an old

---

"Setting an example is not the main means of influencing another, it is the only means."

—ALBERT EINSTEIN

"general store" from years ago. It was packed from floor to ceiling with tools and supplies for "home improvement." I was greeted by a very friendly gentleman, and I learned that this was a family business that had been at this location for decades. The gentleman listened intently as I explained my dilemma. Then, without hesitation, he said, "We can help." As I described each project, the owner did more than just name the items I would need. He actually walked me through the store, showing me every tool that would be essential to the work and carefully explaining exactly how the job should be done. He added, "If you need me to stop by after work and answer any questions or show you how to do anything, just give me a call on my cell phone." Handing me a card, he said, "Here's the number."

I never asked him to come by the house, but I did call on several occasions for advice. He always took time to thoroughly explain what I needed to do. While I felt like a dummy because I had to ask for guidance so frequently, this man was ever gracious and generous with his time and attention. With his help the projects were completed . . . and my wife was very happy! And, thank God, I didn't lose an arm or leg, not even a finger, in the process. Because of his extraordinary service, I have sent scores of would-be handymen to see him.

"There are two types of people who never achieve very much in their life times," says Andrew Carnegie. "One is the person who won't do what he or she is told to do, and the other is the person who does no more than he or she is told to do."[14] Generous people do more than is expected of them. They are "extra mile" people. Believe me, there are no traffic jams on the "extra mile."

Generous people are also others-focused. They have discovered great fulfillment in giving and serving. "There is a route to genuine and enduring satisfaction, but it flies in the face of this greedy, self-obsessed culture. It's called *generosity*, and it involves giving our four most valuable resources—our time, talents, treasure and touch. The generous person will receive unimaginable riches in return."[15]

Many organizations and development representatives present appreciation gifts to their donors *after* a gift has been received. Though I follow that practice faithfully, I am also a strong believer in giving *before* the gift is made so that donors can witness generosity by example. I take a gift bag with me to every meeting with a potential giver and present the gift early on—long before giving is ever mentioned. (I usually offer a couple of books on leadership, stewardship, or discipleship that have genuine potential to add value and blessing to a donor's life.) Whether the individual gives or not, generosity has been sown. And that's what we must do: sow generosity that we may reap generosity. After all, the Bible does say, "Whatever a man sows, that he will also reap" (Gal. 6:7 NKJV).

L.O.V.E. them. *L*isten to your ministry partners. *O*pen your heart to them. *V*alue them. *E*xemplify generosity. In so doing, you will:

- raise their self-esteem as you add value to them;
- raise their generosity as you model generosity before them;
- raise their opinion of Christ as they see Him in you; and
- raise their standard of giving as they follow you, as you follow Christ.

In short, L.O.V.E. them, and you will raise *more than money*!

12

A Closer Look at L.E.A.D. Them

"Write the vision and make it plain on tablets,
that he may run who reads it."
—Habakkuk 2:2 NKJV

In Chapter 11, we discussed the first of four crucial steps to building strong, enduring relationships with ministry partners. We learned that we must *L.O.V.E. them*. In this chapter, we will look at the second phase of the development journey. This phase involves effectively demonstrating leadership in the lives of those you serve. Leadership is servanthood, and you, the development representative, are always to *serve* givers. But leadership is also *influence*. While you must never attempt to pressure anyone into presenting a gift, you *can* be a key influencer in the giving process. As a servant-leader who has built a strong relationship with a generous individual, based on impeccable integrity, you can often guide that individual in the process of making a donation that results in maximum eternal impact.

L.E.A.D. Them

Lay out the dream.
Explain the strategy.
Ask them for partnership.
Deliver what you promise.

The second step is not about arm-twisting. It's about walking beside people who care, traveling with them on the pathway of biblical stewardship, and experiencing with them the unspeakable joy of generous, strategic kingdom giving.

Many representatives of nonprofit organizations think that their key role is to connect givers and potential givers with their organization, to meet *its* needs. In the beginning, I thought the same way. Soon, however, I came to a different conclusion: organizations, even the finest of ministries, do not have needs. *People* have needs! Most Christian ministries, I believe, are genuinely trying to effectively address those needs. Thus, I have concluded that the key role of the development representative and his or her organization is to provide an opportunity for real people to meet real needs in the lives of real people. So, whether the help comes through evangelism, discipleship, leadership training, crisis relief, compassionate ministries, or "other," somewhere in the process we as development representatives must connect human needs with men and women who have the God-given resources necessary to meet those needs. We will have to *L.E.A.D.* them. Here's how:

L – LAY OUT THE DREAM

Effective development representatives are fueled by a vision that sees needs met and lives changed. In many cases that vision began in the mind of a leader whose heart was broken by human suffering. God then used that leader to establish an organization that would develop and implement a strategy to meet the sufferers' needs. The successful development representative has been captured by that mission. It burns in his bones. He detests the status quo.

The development representative must cast the vision clearly, concisely, creatively, consistently, and compellingly. There will likely be discussions with donors and potential donors about dozens of aspects of an organization. However, whatever is discussed, from annual funding to special events to capital campaigns, the organization's vision must be the foundation of every conversation and presentation. The development representative's passion for that vision will be contagious. It inevitably creates interest on the part of givers and potential givers.

Our vision statement at EQUIP reads: "To see effective leaders fulfill the Great Commission in every nation." In our hearts we see the day when the fame and glory of Jesus Christ has been spread to every

---

"Leadership is the transference of vision."[1]

—HAL REED

---

land! The entire EQUIP team embraces this vision that God planted in the heart of Dr. John C. Maxwell. Every member of the team passionately believes that millions of effective, godly leaders must be developed around the world if the nations are to be reached for Christ. This conviction stirs us to action every day . . . causing us to go the second mile to see the dream become a reality.

E – EXPLAIN THE STRATEGY

People will give to a clear vision that focuses on meeting real needs in the lives of people. In fact, vision, I believe, is deeply rooted in seeing needs met. Vision is *why* we do what we do. But vision is nothing without strategy. Strategy is *how* we do what we do. It is closely related to the mission of the organization. EQUIP's mission statement reads: "To equip international Christian leaders to effectively serve the Body of Christ throughout the world." How will we do this? Our "strategy," or *process*, as it says on our Web site is: "To provide strategic leadership training through conferences, resources, partnerships and technology." Put simply, we provide biblical leadership training and resources for Christian leaders worldwide—we train leaders. But we do more than that.

We also train leaders who train leaders who train leaders. We at EQUIP firmly believe in the Law of Explosive Growth as taught by Dr. Maxwell in his book *The 21 Irrefutable Laws of Leadership*. He writes, "To add growth, lead followers—to multiply, lead leaders."[2] Dr. Maxwell calls this principle "leader's math."[3] He explains, "Leaders who develop followers grow their organization only one person at a time. But leaders who develop leaders multiply their growth, because for every leader they develop, they also receive all of the leader's followers."[4]

We at EQUIP believe that Jesus Himself gave us this model. Even though He preached to the multitudes, healed the sick, and engaged in many other ministry activities, clearly He devoted most of His time to developing a team of leaders to whom He could pass the leadership baton.

We, too, are committed to this mission. We do this one thing. We believe it is the key to reaching a lost world for Christ. We refuse to be sidetracked. And though we highly respect all ministries involved in Great Commission work—and faithfully seek ways to add value to them—we exist to *raise up* Christlike leaders. We trust that this mission is changing the world!

Timothy Smith writes:

> When I am face to face with a donor, I have to be able to trust my mission. I have to know it, understand it, and believe it. I have to be committed to it heart and soul. My heart has to beat with the pulse of that mission. Then, every interaction with that donor, every conversation—all the way from chit-chat about casual everyday goings-on to the "moment of truth" when I'm asking for a donation—will flow naturally out of, and back to, that mission. If the rep isn't sold on it, the donor is unlikely to buy into it.[5]

I wholeheartedly agree. And not only must the development rep trust, understand, and believe his mission, but he must also be able to *communicate* that mission. Sometimes that's easier—and more effective—to illustrate than to explain. How is it done? By sharing stories of *changed lives*. Every development representative must become an able teller of stories of how the organization's mission has met people's needs and transformed their lives. In fact, a clear presentation of *what we do* (mission) and *how we do it* (strategy) must accompany every presentation of *why we do what we do* (vision). When a development representative fails at this, it can impede any desire a donor might have had to collaborate with that organization to impact the kingdom. It can spell disaster as you attempt to "close." But if you ignite a fire in the heart of a potential donor—by your enthusiastic communication and passionate storytelling—you are ready to take the next step:

A – ASK FOR PARTNERSHIP

Once you have built a friendship based on trust and have established a relationship around a shared vision, requesting a financial investment will be a natural part of the conversation. It will not seem at all awkward to ask a friend for partnership to make a God-given dream become a reality. But remember: the giver must be seen as a *partner in ministry*, not as a source of income.

When you ask for partnership, view the gift, regardless of size, as just one step on a longer ministry journey together. The "ask" provides opportunity for both the giver and the organization to commit specific resources to solving a problem. In part, the organization provides strategy, expertise, experience, and personnel. The giver commits financial resources, prayer, and perhaps volunteer work. The commitment is about doing ministry together.

The request for partnership must contain a sense of urgency. I am not talking about arm-twisting, sales-pitchy pressure, or a contrived crisis in order to raise funds. (Even a bank robber could be called a fund-raiser!) Development work is *not* fund-raising. It is partnership building for the purpose of making an eternally significant difference—together!

The partnership request must also clearly convey the difference that one's donation can make in meeting the *real* needs of *real* people. Bill Sturtevant in *The Artful Journey* tells of a donor who interrupted his presentation of a building project. "Bill," he said, "I've built plenty of buildings during my career. You don't need to tell me about the number of windows and rooms. What I want you to tell me about are the people who will pass through the halls of the building and what they will accomplish. I am far more interested in what goes on inside a building than I am with the structural details."[6] The financial request is not about dollars; it is about giving to change lives. The "ask" must underscore the impact the gift will make by the results it will produce.

So what is the best way to request a gift? How does a development representative go about it? The most effective "ask" must be *personal*, *passionate*, and *purposeful*. To elaborate, requests for giving should be made face-to-face, with a sense of urgency, and should spell out clearly the difference that the donor's gift will make. Furthermore, the request should never place limits on the giver. In other words, talk freely about the size and scope of the need. Be honest. Ask largely. And don't second-guess.

When I served as the director of a mission school for Native Americans, the governing board gave us permission to develop a modern high school campus provided *we* raised the funds needed. I will never forget my first visit in the home of a wealthy gentleman. I was young, with almost no experience in development work. I was very uncomfortable as I discussed our immediate necessity: a specific building. We urgently needed $80,000, but when he asked what the school needed, I panicked and blurted out *$500*. He gave me a check for $500. I have no idea why I said that except that I was under pressure and extremely stressed discussing such a large need with a man I hardly knew. Nothing seemed natural about the conversation. Thankfully, a few days later this dear gentleman telephoned me. He said, "Because you are young and need to learn an important lesson,

I'm going to give you a second opportunity to tell the truth about your need." After a few seconds of silence, he added, "*What do you need?*"

"Eighty thousand dollars for a building" I answered in a whisper.

"Speak up!" he ordered.

This time, with more volume, I repeated, "*Eighty thousand dollars.*"

He chuckled and said, "I thought you'd never ask. I'll take care of the building. You'll receive a check soon."

"If there is something to gain and nothing to lose by asking, by all means ask!"

—W. CLEMENT STONE, BEST-SELLING AUTHOR AND FOUNDER OF COMBINED INSURANCE CO.

I don't think I need to explain how much I learned that day about the importance of asking honestly, without second-guessing.

Let me also highlight the weight of persistence in the development process. Relationship building is not instant. It takes time. If you ask for partnership and receive a negative response, the "no" often just means "not now." Don't drop the ball. Continue with your efforts to build the relationship.

I recall vividly my first visit with an Arizona gentleman who was known for his generous support of evangelical causes. He very graciously agreed to meet me for lunch at his favorite Mexican restaurant, a little mom-and-pop café not far from his office.

As we enjoyed tacos and enchiladas, we shared our personal testimonies of faith in Christ. He told me about his family and business. I told him about how God had led me to ministry with Native American youth. He kindly asked me about my dreams for the future of our ministry.

When I mentioned our need for funds to construct a building, he reached across the table and took my hand. "I have already committed major financial resources to a couple of ministries over the next few years," he said. "I simply cannot be of help at this point . . . but let me pray for you and your family." After he had asked God to grant us favor and supply our every need, he said, "I appreciate your passion to reach Indian youth for Christ. Come and see me again about this time next year."

Each year for the next eight years I phoned this Christian businessman and asked if we could meet for lunch. Each year we met in the same restaurant and consumed lots of tacos and enchiladas. Each year he asked me for an update on our ministry and about our most pressing needs. And each year I asked him to partner with us to reach Indian youth with the gospel. Eight times he prayed for the youth we

---

"Most of the important things in the world have been accomplished by people who have kept on trying when there seemed to be no hope at all."

—DALE CARNEGIE

---

served and for me, expressing thanks for the ministry. Then he explained that he could not be helpful at that time.

On our ninth visit we sat in the very same booth where I first met him. We had now known each other for almost a decade. After he asked God's blessing upon our food, he looked me in the eye and said, "It is now time for me to invest in your ministry to American Indian young people. Do you have a project for me?" As I explained the need for a particular building, he interrupted me. "How much will it cost for a turnkey job done by a qualified contractor?" I cited the latest estimate that had been given to me, and the name of the contractor.

"I trust that builder," he replied. "Please call me tomorrow with the exact cost of the building. I will cover the cost. My assistant will have a check in your hands within thirty days." Ten days later the check arrived with a note thanking me for staying in touch with him about our ministry and giving him an opportunity to make a difference in the lives of Native American youth.

I strongly believe in inviting God's people to give generously to His work. Asking believers who have been blessed with financial resources to make major gifts to kingdom work is in tune with the biblical mandate to become faithful stewards of the resources placed in their care. Giving pleases God and brings joy to the giver. But don't ask—*never* ask, unless you have committed to . . .

D – DELIVER WHAT YOU PROMISE

Implicit in the "ask" is a promise that the funds given will bring about a specific result. This is where you must be ever so careful. So many times development representatives, eager to receive a gift, have promised a greater outcome than the gift could possibly produce. I would much rather *under*promise and *over*deliver! What a joy to be able to report to a giver that his gift has produced *better*-than-expected results.

It has been my experience that many first-time gifts are made based on the giver's confidence in the solicitor's, not the organization's, integrity. The development rep's *own* character is the major factor in whether the giver believes the promises made by the representative. But if an initial gift is to become the first of many to an organization, another factor comes into play: competence. The organization must gain the giver's unwavering confidence in its ability to do what was promised. *Guarantees* must turn into *results*, and these must be accurate and honestly communicated to the giver.

Character and competence—coupled with honest and regular communication—are crucial to building and maintaining strong, effective, long-lasting partnerships.

On those occasions when, for whatever reason, the results anticipated were not achieved, you *must* provide a complete and timely explanation to the donor. Likewise, if there has been a delay in utilizing the funds, whatever the cause, the giver must be informed. Givers don't expect organizations to be perfect, but they do expect organizational leaders to be honest—100 percent of the time! This is how you *L.E.A.D.* them. You *honestly* lay out the dream—God's dream—that you and your organization hope to achieve for the kingdom. Then you explain your strategy . . . *honestly*. You ask for a partnership to implement your strategy, being—here's that word again—*honest* about your project needs. And finally, you deliver what you promised . . . because you and your organization are *honest*. What was it that Shakespeare said? "Honesty is the best policy"? It is if you want to *raise more than money*—and accomplish God's dreams.

13

A Closer Look at L.I.N.K. Them

"You can do what I cannot do. I can do what you cannot do. Together, we can do great things."

—Mother Teresa

So far we've looked at two phases of the development process. In phase I, we learned to *L.O.V.E. them*, listening to our potential partners and opening our hearts to them. In this stage, we discovered that we must value them as persons, not providers, and that before ever expecting generosity from them, we must first model it ourselves. In short, phase I was about making *friendships*.

In phase II, we learned how to *L.E.A.D. them*. We laid out the dream in which we want donors to take an active part. Then, after explaining our intended strategy, we asked them to partner *with* us, ensuring that for every promise we make, we deliver. In this phase, we made *connections* with people—*relationships*—based on a common *vision*.

Phase III in the development process is about an ever-stronger *partnership* that is focused on doing ministry together for utmost kingdom impact. While the results of the partnership will become increasingly important, the relational aspect must never be overlooked. In phase III we will endeavor to . . .

L.I.N.K. Them

<u>L</u>ift them up in prayer.
<u>I</u>nvolve them.
<u>N</u>ever take them for granted.
<u>K</u>eep them informed.

L – Lift Them Up in Prayer

The family that prays together stays together is an assertion that those in Christian circles have heard countless times. I believe it's true. I also believe strongly that the leaders of ministry organizations must faithfully pray for their financial partners because they are family too. Every time a development representative visits with a giver, prayer should be a vital part of the meeting. Whenever I talk with a giver—whether face-to-face or by phone—I always ask that individual to give me the privilege to pray for him or her. I encourage the donor to share specific prayer requests with me and to keep me updated. And because I am sincere about this, every donor has not only my e-mail address, but my cell phone number. If you are sincere when asking a giver to keep you informed about a prayer concern, don't make it next to impossible for the donor to contact you.

Several months ago, when Dr. John Hull, president/CEO of EQUIP, asked me to take on more general administrative responsibilities and to oversee our special initiatives in China, I accepted the role of senior vice president. Though I continue to work closely with many of our key givers, our development activities are now guided by Mr. Dan Glaze. Dan, whom I call "Mr. Relationships," brought to EQUIP a track record of proven effectiveness in development. But what I most admire about Dan is his genuine love and concern for our donors. Regardless of the pressure he is under or the deadlines he is facing, Dan's chief ministry priority each day is to lift our constituents in prayer. It doesn't surprise me at all that Dan has very quickly built strong relationships with many friends of this ministry.

Another way to keep prayer at the forefront with donors is to include prayer request forms with mailings to your constituents. Encourage them regularly to telephone or e-mail the ministry with urgent prayer requests. When requests are received, organizational

---

"A lot of kneeling will keep you in good standing."

—AUTHOR UNKNOWN

---

leaders and staff must be faithful to pray. In our office, when we receive word of a crisis situation, it is not unusual for us to interrupt work to call everyone together for prayer. Otherwise, requests are communicated to staff by e-mail. Every Monday morning our entire staff meets for prayer. We always intercede on behalf of those who give to make possible the worldwide ministry of EQUIP.

Individually, I encourage development representatives to pray daily for a group of their givers, lifting them by name before the Lord.

I – INVOLVE THEM

If I could offer only one word of advice to nonprofit organizations, it would be: Involve your givers in hands-on ministry. When organizational leaders see their donors as friends and partners, not as sources of revenue, they search for meaningful ways to involve them in the ministry, to *link* them—physically, even—to achieving the mission.

When I served as director of a residential Christian school for Native American children in Arizona, it was crystal clear that we did not have adequate funds to hire all the necessary staff. So my coworkers and I communicated to our donors our need for volunteers to fill a variety of roles. We had openings for volunteer secretaries, classroom tutors, cooks, dorm supervisors, coaches, maintenance workers, you name it. At the same time, we were usually involved in a building project that required the skills of large numbers of volunteers.

I served this school for sixteen years, and every year the number of volunteers increased. During my last school year (1979–80), there were more than sixty volunteers, not counting groups of them who worked on construction projects. And in almost every case, when a donor volunteered, his or her level of giving steadily increased, often dramatically. Most of our top givers were also volunteers.

As mentioned previously, EQUIP was launched in 1996. From 1996 to 2001 the ministry experienced steady growth in gift income, with donors involved only at the giving level. But in 2002 we decided to offer our financial partners the opportunity to become involved at another level—as volunteer associate trainers. In addition to financially contributing to EQUIP, donors would be asked to complete training in the EQUIP curriculum *and* to commit to travel overseas twice yearly for three years—six international trips *at their own expense*—to teach biblical leadership principles on a volunteer basis. A recent study indicates that these same volunteer teachers, now training Christian leaders in more than one hundred nations on five continents, compose the overwhelming majority of the chief donors to EQUIP.

N – Never Take Them for Granted

Relationships, like flowers, die if they are not faithfully cultivated. Honest and frequent communication is the key. A married couple can live in the same house, yet have no meaningful relationship because they fail to communicate. On the other hand, individuals living on opposite sides of the planet can maintain a strong friendship by frequently using the means of communication available to them. Telephone, e-mail, and other technologies enable those who are geographically separated to remain relationally close.

As I have visited the homes and offices of hundreds of givers through the years, I have been amazed at the countless stories of organizations that ignore their donors. While visiting with a gentleman in Oregon many years ago, I handed him a couple of books as I expressed my gratitude for his faithful and generous support. As I updated him on the lives that were being changed by his gifts, he interrupted me and said, "I can't believe you are here. I give very generously

---

"The deepest craving of human nature
is the need to be appreciated."

— WILLIAM JAMES

---

to five ministries, but I have never had anyone stop by to see me. They only write me or call me when they are asking for more money." I've heard similar comments dozens of times from donors who feel ignored by the ministries they support.

My friendship deepened with this Oregonian giver as we communicated regularly through face-to-face meetings, phone calls, e-mails, and short, handwritten notes. The relationship became so strong that he would often call and say, "It's time for me to give again." Over the years he gave several million dollars to the organization I represented.

The donor "dropout" rate is very high in most organizations. I believe this high attrition is primarily the fault of the organization. The leadership of nonprofit ministries must make ministry to donors (thanking them, informing them, serving them, investing in them) a high priority, committing time and resources to this vital process. It must be intentional.

Acknowledge gifts promptly. A phone call and a handwritten note following the receipt of a gift are vital first steps in maintaining a strong and growing relationship. And finally . . .

K – KEEP THEM INFORMED

Keep your givers up to date with frequent and accurate reports. Use every available means to ensure that your givers know exactly what their partnership with your organization is accomplishing. Communicate often. Communicate honestly. And communicate diversely. To accomplish that for our givers, EQUIP has constructed a Web site that is innovative, inspirational, informative, and interactive. The latest ministry news is posted regularly on the site. Not only that, but visitors to the site can download resources, view video presentations, read Q&As, and even interact with pastors and leaders worldwide. Make updating your partners interesting for them—it will be profitable for you.

Each quarter we send our major donors a CD presentation known as the Global Stage. It contains a timely interview by our president with a key international leader. It also includes up-to-the-minute news from EQUIP ministries around the world.

Our givers also receive a quarterly newsletter. Further, we produce and distribute at least one new DVD each year, focused on a continent or key nation where EQUIP is training leaders. And we host complimentary luncheons, known as executive briefings, to which we invite our donors. Each luncheon focuses on a specific nation or region of the world. Our recent briefings have been related to Iraq, Iran, Lebanon, and China.

All of our donors receive personal visits, phone calls, e-mails, and handwritten notes just to say thanks and to keep them current on the latest EQUIP news. We also give them opportunities to travel overseas with EQUIP personnel to see the ministry in action. In August 2006, I received the following e-mail from Vincent Hungate, executive director of Essential2Life. It illustrates the importance of the relational funding concept.

> I just wanted to follow up with you and say thank you for the time that you spent with me almost a year ago. I consider you a friend and a mentor. Your wisdom and insight when it comes to relational funding has changed Essential2life for the good. Just a quick update on our finances—we grew almost 33 percent in our year-end giving and have already set a record pace for this fiscal year. We

have doubled our yearly budget and are on course for making it. I wanted to see when you would be back in town so we could connect again. I look forward to hearing back from you soon and getting together.[1]

Why does my friend and partner want to get together again? Because we didn't fail to *L.I.N.K.* him with us. Vincent knows he can count on me to *lift him up in prayer*. He is *involved* with our ministry. He knows that we at EQUIP *never take him and his organization for granted*. And we have taken the time to *keep him informed*—and as you can see, he is doing the same.

14

A Closer Look at L.I.F.T. Them

There is no exercise better for the heart than reaching out and lifting people up.

—Author unknown

In the previous chapters, we have learned three critical phases in the relational funding process. To establish strong, open relationships with donors, over the "long haul," we have learned that we must *L.O.V.E.* them as friends, *L.E.A.D.* them in relationship, and *L.I.N.K.* them with us as partners to achieve multiplied results. Phase IV in the development process involves four steps to help the giver practice biblical stewardship. This stage is about stewardship as, not an event, but a lifestyle. It is about giving from accumulated assets, not just from cash flow.

Having served donors for the past four decades, I have learned that less than 10 percent of one's assets are in the form of cash. Most of what we possess is in real estate, personal goods, and other investments. Biblical stewards know that 100 percent of their holdings belong to God and that they are accountable to Him for everything He has placed in their care. They begin to dream about gifts that will have major kingdom impact both now and for generations to come.

This final stage of the development journey is all about investing in givers and lifting them to levels of kingdom involvement that will meet—and exceed—their dreams of making an eternal difference, and in so doing, they will accomplish *God's* dreams. How will we do this? We will . . .

L.I.F.T THEM

<u>L</u>isten to them . . . (*again!*).
<u>I</u>nvest in them.
<u>F</u>acilitate their dreams.
<u>T</u>hank them often.

L – LISTEN TO THEM

Sound familiar? Yes, *listening* was also the first step in phase I. Why is listening so important? Because "the most basic of all human needs is the need to . . . be understood. The best way to understand people is to listen to them."[1] As development representatives, we need to ask key givers about their dreams as parents and as biblical stewards. We must listen as they talk about their aspirations for their children, their grandchildren, their churches, and the organizations that are important to them. Only then can we lovingly, gently, and wisely help them find answers to important questions such as these: *How much should I bequeath to my loved ones? When should it be done—and how? What are some ways I can decrease taxes and increase my giving to kingdom causes? How can I give more* now, *instead of waiting until my death?*

To gain the knowledge to effectively aid donors in answering these questions, we first must . . .

I – INVEST IN THEM

A sincere biblical steward can be full of questions—such as:

- What portion of my income do I need for a lifestyle that honors Christ while providing adequately for my family?

- How do I most effectively "lay up treasures in heaven"?
- When and how should I begin to give away my accumulated assets?
- Do I need to establish a foundation or a donor-advised fund?
- How will I deal with business succession issues?

At EQUIP we offer books, videos, and other resources that will help answer the critical questions that biblical stewards must address. Each quarter we also publish a very informative newsletter that deals

---

"The most basic of all human needs is the need to . . .
be understood. The best way to understand
people is to listen to them."

—RALPH NICHOLS

---

with estate and gift design. This newsletter is written by Mr. Ray Lyne, the foremost authority on estate and gift planning. Downloadable information is available at no cost from our Web site. We also make our donors aware of other Web sites and live seminars that specialize in responding to these issues from a Christian perspective.

Provide your donors with resources that help them understand that money, from God's perspective, is simply a means to hasten His redemptive mission on the earth. This biblical understanding of money and possessions frees us from a preoccupation with financial wealth. Money is not seen as power; neither is it seen as sinful or *"the root of all evil!"* as described by the radio preacher I mentioned in the introduction to this book. As God's stewards, we understand that money is helpful with life's necessities and its enjoyments, but we see much more. We view money as a God-endowed instrument for advancing His cause in the world.

F – FACILITATE THEIR DREAMS

At EQUIP, it is our joy to arrange for our major donors to meet privately with Ray Lyne to discuss estate and gift design. There is no cost to our friends. Ray never pressures them to give to EQUIP. He simply answers stewardship questions from a biblical perspective. That's because Ray doesn't serve EQUIP; he serves God's people and helps them carry out their charitable-gift desires as wise stewards of their God-given resources.

Every organization should provide endowment opportunities for men and women who want to bestow gifts that will "keep on giving" after their donors are promoted to heaven. We typically think of these enduring gifts in connection with wills and bequests, given after one's death. But many people can contribute generously through their estate plans *and* in this lifetime. Development representatives should encourage God's people to make generous contributions while they are still alive.

Kennon L. Callahan, in his book, *Effective Church Finances*, cautions churches and other ministries to select endowment projects carefully: "Select projects that have integrity and long-term value," he writes. "Thus, for example, we would not have as an endowment project the building of a tool shed out back. We would not endow a project that has so narrow a focus that it might not have lasting value. You want projects that have an enduring character with flexibility and creativity for the future."[2]

If you are truly committed to serving the giver and listening well to his or her dreams, you will choose your endowments wisely. There may also be occasions when, as a representative, you are called upon to connect donors with *other* excellent ministries that fit their desires to make a difference in a specialized arena of ministry. Again, choose wisely.

And finally—and we cannot stress this enough . . .

T – Thank Them Often

Gratitude is the underpinning of every contact with givers. For more than forty years in ministry, I have stopped every morning to thank God for prayer and financial partners in Great Commission work.

"I would maintain that thanks are the highest form of thought, and that gratitude is happiness doubled by wonder."

—G. K. Chesterton

Each day it is my commitment to express gratitude—in person, by phone, through e-mail, or by a note in my own hand—to several faithful, generous Christian stewards. Many of them interrupt me as I am trying to express gratitude to say things like, "No, let me thank *you* and EQUIP for giving me the opportunity to make investments that are making a difference for the kingdom of God." When grateful people connect with grateful people, the result is a powerful partnership that affects eternity.

So now you have learned the four critical processes that every development representative needs to perform to convert potential givers into biblical stewards: *L.O.V.E.* them, *L.E.A.D.* them, *L.I.N.K.* them, and *L.I.F.T.* them. Only by engaging in these vital *relationship-building* steps can you hope to—in concert with your partners—accomplish God's dreams. That's because, to rehearse the words of Margaret Wheatley, quoted in the introduction to part III, "relationships are all there is." We must create them, we must build them, and we must maintain them. In Chapter 15 we will discuss keys to maintaining the strong relationships that you must forge as you engage in *raising more than money*.

15

Keys to Maintaining Strong Relationships

Care is the ingredient that keeps true friendships alive despite separation, distance, or time.

— Sara Paddison, *Hidden Power of the Heart*

By now you are convinced that development work is *not* fund-raising. It is, instead, the *ministry* of helping the body of Christ know the thrill of not only living in an *intimate relationship* but also a *financial partnership* with the Father. In light of this discovery, all of your development work should be evaluated with these three questions in mind:

- Have I covered my work *every day* with prayer?
- Do I show integrity and accountability?
- Am I seeking the giver's spiritual benefit?

This is important because *every* financial partner, from the one who sends a dollar a month to the six-digit donor, deserves your wholehearted effort and concern. This is the only way you can ever hope to effect true relational funding from *all* of your partners.

THE KEY PLAYERS

But every ministry support team needs some *key* players—partners who give generously, usually in larger amounts, *and* who are able and willing to influence others to give. To develop and maintain strong relationships with these kinds of players—and every other, for that matter—requires that you keep several key issues in mind:

Results. People live—and give—for results. So, as you share your vision with ministry partners, talk about the future *results*. What does your organization hope to achieve? What will your donors' gifts effect? Whose lives will their giving change? In short, what will *result* from their contributions? Make sure you, as motivational speaker Gary Ryan Blair puts it, "connect today's actions with tomorrow's results."[1]

Competence. Donors must have confidence that we can do what we promise—and can do it well.

Trust. Not only must donors be confident that we *can* do what we promise, but that we *will* do what we promise. We must earn their trust, because trust is the key to all relationship building. Trust, in fact, "is a fundamental precondition for all successful fundraising," say authors Jeavon and Basinger, "and should be a hallmark in all relationships among Christians . . . Trust has to be evident for everyone as they trust in God's generosity and faithfulness; for donors, as they trust in an organization's integrity and reliability; and among fundraisers and organization leaders, as they trust in donors' judgment."[2]

Once you have gained a donor's trust, handle it with care. Don't make promises your organization can't keep, because trust, once lost, is hard to regain. Someone once said, "Trust is like a vase—once it's broken, though you can fix it, the vase will never be the same again." Worse, sometimes it can't be fixed at all.

Significance. According to American Values Coach Joe Tye, "The REAL American Dream is not about a garage full of new cars, winning the lottery, or retiring to a life of ease in Florida. It's about doing work that has meaning, work that makes a difference."[3] Your ministry partners have the same dream: they, too, want to make a difference—an *eternal* difference. You must assure them that, by partnering with your organization, they will.

Relationships. A donor wants to be valued as a person, not as a source of funds. Listen to your donors. Invest time and resources in them. Find ways to serve them. Be generous in "giving back" to them.

Results. No, this is not a typo. Begin *and* end with results. Ministry partners want to know what was accomplished with their investments.

"Trust is like a vase—once it's broken, though you can fix it, the vase will never be the same again."

—AUTHOR UNKNOWN

We don't have to bat a thousand, but whatever our batting average is, we must frequently and *accurately* report it. That means no exaggerating or inflating the numbers. Exaggeration, wrote nineteenth-century poet Eliza Cook "offends the perceptive."[4]

OBSERVATIONS FROM WORKING WITH MAJOR DONORS

On Mutual Respect: Large gifts are almost always preceded by a relationship based on trust and mutual respect.

On Flexibility: There must be flexibility in determining when gifts will be made and for what purpose(s).

On Face-to-Face Appeals: Larger gifts usually follow face-to-face visits.

On Being "You" Focused: To effect large-scale giving, your appeal must be "you" focused, not "my ministry" focused. Appeal to the "you" you are speaking to—the ministry partner—and show how he or she can meet real needs in the lives of real people.

RELATIONAL MAINTENANCE TIPS

1. Visit your ministry partners regularly. Invest your time in them.
2. Invite donors to visit your ministry.
3. Ask givers for advice; then *listen* to them.
4. Take ministry partners to see the projects in which they have invested.
5. Send donors personally signed cards on their birthdays and anniversaries.
6. Send gifts—books, CDs, music, articles, etc.—that will add value to givers' lives.
7. Keep your ministry partners informed by reporting to them regularly.
8. Thank donors promptly, personally, and frequently (by cards, letters, e-mails, phone calls, and personal visits).
9. Send givers copies of your media releases.
10. Use videos, DVDs, etc., to give your ministry partners "up close" looks at their gifts in action.
11. Make every request a thank-you.
12. Invite donors to special events.
13. Always err on the side of generosity.
14. Pray regularly for givers.

The Carnegie Technological Institute has stated that 90 percent of all people who fail in their life's vocation fail because they cannot get along with people.[5] In closing this chapter, I submit to you ten simple ways to improve your relational skills so that you, the development officer, can *raise more than money*.

Ten Commandments of Human Relations

1. Speak to people. There is nothing as nice as a cheerful word of greeting.
2. Smile at people. It takes seventy-two muscles to frown, only fourteen to smile.
3. Call people by name. Music to anyone's ears is the sound of his/her own name.
4. Be friendly and helpful.
5. Be cordial. Speak and act as if everything you do is genuinely a pleasure, and if it isn't, learn to make it so.
6. Be genuinely interested in people. You can like almost everybody if you try.
7. Be generous with praise, cautious with criticism.
8. Be considerate with the feelings of others. There are usually three sides to a controversy: yours, the other fellow's, and the right one.
9. Be alert to serve. What counts most in life is what we do for others.
10. Add to this a good sense of humor, a huge dose of patience and a dash of humility.[6]

16

Life Is About Relationships

Man is a knot . . . into which relationships are tied.

—Antoine de Saint-Exupéry, *Flight to Arras*

Peter Senge, author of *The Fifth Discipline* and director of the Center for Organizational Learning at MIT's Sloan School of Management, is emphatic about the importance of relationships. "As we enter the twenty-first century," he wrote, "it is timely, perhaps even critical, that we recall what human beings have understood for a very long time. Working together can indeed be a deep source of life meaning. Anything less is just a job."[1]

By now I hope it is your firm conviction that development work done God's way is not about raising money. It's about raising people into the likeness of Jesus Christ, so that they will be in right *relationship* with God. See, when God the Father sees His Son in *us*, our *relationship* with Him will be sound. That's because He recognizes, reflected in us as we give to kingdom work, the *very* nature of our benevolent Savior.

For from him and through him and to him are all things.
To him be the glory forever! Amen. (Rom. 11:36 NIV)

I love the way Kennon Callahan describes the wonderful privilege of giving. In *Effective Church Finances*, he writes:

> Giving is grace. The reward is the giving. As we live, we grow. We become newer, deeper people. Our sense of confidence and trust grows. Our sense of vision and hope grows.
>
> It is not "when you give, God will reward you" thinking. The reward is the giving. As you give, you share God's grace. The act of giving is virtually a sacrament of grace. The act of giving is both a sign and an event of the generosity of God in our lives. In this sense, the act of giving is the sharing of God's grace.
>
> The event of giving is like the break of a new day, with the sun sharing its life-giving warmth. The event of giving is like a gentle rain that gives new life to the earth and all who dwell therein. Giving is like the discovery of two friends that they love one another deeply and dearly. Giving has a warmth, a wonder, a grace about it. Giving is deeper than the oceans, higher than the mountains, more enduring than the earth. Giving is remembered long and well. Giving is its own reward.[2]

Until the day she died, my mom lived out the truth that the act of giving is sharing God's grace. I mentioned earlier that I lost my father when I was eleven and my sister only eight. Because Dad died a few months short of the date when his wife and children would be eligible for survivor's benefits, Mom was penniless. To support us, she took a minimum-wage job in the kitchen of the local high school.

Yet, as she brought up two children on a very limited income, Mom never failed to give more than 10 percent of her income to the church and to generously support both a Bible college and several missionaries. She also volunteered countless hours to compassionate ministries in her community. When she finally retired, she became a self-supporting missionary to Indians in Arizona, serving there about ten years. She spent her final years pretty much confined to her home following a debilitating stroke.

I remember calling her one morning not too long before her promotion to heaven. When I asked about her condition, she replied, "My body is weak, but I've never been more alive. I am truly the most blessed person on earth. This morning I read my Bible, a love letter

---

"Giving is deeper than the oceans, higher than the mountains, more enduring than the earth. Giving is remembered long and well. Giving is its own reward."

—KENNON CALLAHAN

---

from my Father; then, on the wings of prayer, I visited about twenty-five countries as I interceded for missionaries I love. Then I wrote gift checks to my church, a mission agency, and a Christian college. Without leaving my room, because of the wonderful privileges of prayer and giving, today I have touched the face of God, wrapped my arms around a lost world, and invested in the next generation of Christian leaders. My heart overflows with joy!"

May your heart also overflow with joy as you give generously—and lead others to do the same—and may God's face shine upon all of your relationships, with your family, your friends, your ministry partners, and most of all, with His Son. Life is about relationships. May yours be blessed as you seek with all your heart to *accomplish God's dreams*!

Notes

Chapter 1—The Heart of the Matter

1. Mark Vincent, *A Christian View of Money* (Scottsdale, AZ: Herald Press, 1997), 9.
2. Paul J. Meyer, *Unlocking Your Legacy: 25 Keys for Success* (Chicago: Moody, 2003), 26.
3. C. Bishop, "Such Love," verse 1, *Sing to the Lord* songbook (Kansas City: Lillenas Publishing Company, 1996), 21.
4. Wayne Myers, *Living Beyond the Possible* (McLean, VA: Evangeline Press, 2003), 24–26.
5. John C. Maxwell, *Today Matters: 12 Daily Practices to Guarantee Tomorrow's Success* (New York: Time Warner Book Group, 2004), 248.

Chapter 2—Our Response to God's Extravagant Love

1. Isaac Watts, "When I Survey the Wondrous Cross," verse 4, *Sing to the Lord*, 62.
2. Stan and Linda Toler, *The Cycle of Victorious Giving: Your Time, Your Talent, Your Treasure* (Kansas City: Beacon Hill Press, 2004), 50.
3. Ibid., 51.
4. John Wesley, "The Use of Money," sermon 50 in the standard numbering, http://new.gbgm-umc.org/umhistory/wesley/sermons/50/.

Chapter 3—The Link Between Faith and Possessions

1. George Hester, from a seminar at EQUIP Founders Weekend, August 1999.

2. Wesley K. Willmer, *God and Your Stuff: The Vital Link Between Your Possessions and Your Soul* (Colorado Springs: NavPress, 2002), 44–45.
3. Ibid.
4. Toler and Toler, *The Cycle of Victorious Giving*, 32–33.
5. Randy Alcorn, *The Law of Rewards: Giving What You Can't Keep to Gain What You Can't Lose* (Wheaton, IL: Tyndale House, 2003), 36.
6. Dave Anderson, "Are You Just Making Money, or Are You Making a Difference?" editorial on www.learntolead.com. On this Web page, a visitor can register free of charge to access articles by Dave Anderson.
7. Adapted from Robert Morris, *The Blessed Life* (Ventura, CA: Regal Books, 2002), 56.
8. Ed Owens, Testimony delivered at the annual Generous Giving Conference, Pasadena, CA, February 28–March 2, 2003, www.generousgiving.org/articles/display.asp?id=83.
9. Ibid.

Chapter 4—Personal Stories from Today's Christian Stewards

1. Bernard Palmer, *Wings of Blue Bird* (Fort Valley, GA: Blue Bird Body Company, 1977), 14.
2. Matt's brother, Craig, left Habersham in 1984 to begin a very successful business in retail furniture sales. Craig is also a devout Christian and a generous giver.
3. Matt Eddy, www.habershamdesigns.com/habershamstory_furn.html.
4. Maxwell, *Today Matters*, 110.
5. If you would like to learn more about Ray Lyne and Lifestyle Giving, Inc., visit www.lifestylegiving.com.
6. Alan Gotthardt, *The Eternity Portfolio* (Wheaton, IL: Tyndale House, 2003), 135.
7. Ibid.
8. Todd Duncan, testimonial letter to EQUIP, available at: www.iequip.org/site/c.gqLTIoOBKpF/b.851501/k.98A0/Living_Legacy.htm.
9. Ibid.

Chapter 5—The Joy of Giving

1. Paul Meyer, *Unlocking Your Legacy*, 152.
2. Randy Alcorn, *The Law of Rewards*, 119.

Introduction to Part II

1. Brian Bergstein, AP Business Writer, Saturday, January 13, 2001, Palo Alto, CA (AP), "Hewlett-Packard Co.," Google, Newspaper article.
2. *The American Heritage College Dictionary*, 4th ed., s.v. "Partnership."
3. Bergstein, "Hewlett-Packard Co."

Chapter 6—The Purpose and Principles of Partnership

1. John C. Maxwell, *Winning with People* (Nashville: Thomas Nelson, 2004), 256.
2. John C. Maxwell, *The 17 Indisputable Laws of Teamwork* (Nashville: Thomas Nelson, 2001), 3.
3. Procter and Gamble, "Our History," www.pg.com.
4. *Wikipedia*, s.vv. "Abbott and Costello," www.wikipedia.com.
5. John C. Maxwell, *Leadership Promises* (Nashville: Thomas Nelson, 2003), 195.
6. Shel Horowitz, "How to Make Partnerships Work," www.umass.edu/fambiz/partnership_charter.htm.

Chapter 7—The Power of Partnership

1. *Wikipedia*, s.vv. "Snowball effect," www.wikipedia.com.
2. John Hull, "From the President's Desk, *The Million Leaders Mandate* (MLM newsletter), Winter 2004.

Chapter 8—Pastors and Partnership

1. "The Top Ten Ways to Increase Giving to Your Congregation," www.churchstuff.com/ten.html.
2. Kennon L. Callahan, *Giving and Stewardship in an Effective Church: A Guide for Every Member* (San Francisco: Jossey-Bass, 1992), 75.

3. Ibid., 76.

4. Kennon L. Callahan, *Effective Church Finances: Fund-raising and Budgeting for Church Leaders*, repr. (San Francisco: HarperSanFrancisco, 1992; San Francisco: Jossey-Bass, 1997), 4. Citations are to the Jossey-Bass edition.

5. Ibid., 5.

6. Ibid., 15.

7. Dick Towner, "Ten Questions for Dick Towner of Willow Creek Association," *Empowering Ministries* (a Christian Stewardship Association online publication), www.stewardship.org/resources/Fund_Articles/towner_art.html.

8. Callahan, *Giving and Stewardship*, 15.

Chapter 9—The Pitfalls of Partnership

1. "Biography for Bud Abbott," IMDb, www.imdb.com/name/nm0007941/bio.

2. "A Short History of Dino," www.linevision.com/bio.htm.

3. Susan Pulliam and Almar Latour, "WorldCom Scandal," *Wall Street Journal*, January 12, 2005.

4. Louie Bustle (director of World Missions, Church of the Nazarene), e-mail message to EQUIP.

Introduction to Part III

1. Tim Elmore, ed., Million Leaders Mandate curriculum, workbook 1 (Duluth, GA: EQUIP, n.d.), 122.

2. Keith Ferrazzi, *Never Eat Alone: And Other Secrets to Success, One Relationship at a Time* (New York: Doubleday, 2005), front cover jacket.

3. Margaret Wheatley, *Finding Our Way: Leadership for an Uncertain Time* (San Francisco: Berrett-Koehler Publishers, 2005).

4. Martin and Diedre Bobgan, *How to Counsel from Scripture* (Chicago: Moody Press, 1985), 18.

5. Alfred de Grazia, "Human Nature and Behavior-Cultural Discipline and Speech Divergence," www.quantavolution.org/vol_07/homoschizo_2_06.htm.

Chapter 10—Relational Funding: An Overview

1. Thomas H. Jeavons and Rebekah Burch Basinger, *Growing Givers' Hearts* (San Francisco: Jossey-Bass, 2000), 3.

2. Daryl Heald, "The Heart of Fund-Raising," *Focus on Accountability Newsletter*, Fourth Quarter 2004, ECFA, Winchester, VA.

3. Andy Stanley, *Fields of Gold* (Wheaton, IL: Tyndale House, 2004), 122.

4. Jeavons and Basinger, *Growing Givers' Hearts*, 53.

Chapter 11—A Closer Look at L.O.V.E. Them

1. John R. Frank, *The Ministry of Development: An Introduction to the Strategies for Success in Christian Ministries* (Dallas: EDM Press, 1996), 9.

2. Timothy Smith, *Donors Are People Too: Managing Relationships with Your Ministry's Major Contributors* (Akron, OH: Berkey, Brendel, Sheline, 2003), 14.

3. Ibid., 6–7.

4. William T. Sturtevant, *The Artful Journey: Cultivating and Soliciting the Major Gift* (Chicago: Bonus Books, 1997), 141.

5. Ibid., 143.

6. Mark Sanborn, *The Fred Factor: How Passion in Your Work and Life Can Turn the Ordinary into the Extraordinary* (New York: Doubleday, 2004), 46.

7. John C. Maxwell and Les Parrott, *25 Ways to Win with People: How to Make Others Feel Like a Million Bucks* (Nashville: Thomas Nelson, 2005), 104.

8. Ibid.

9. Ibid.

10. Ibid., 99.

11. Sanborn, *The Fred Factor* (New York: Doubleday, 2004), 46.

12. Maxwell and Parrott, *25 Ways to Win with People*, 123.

13. Stan Toler and Martha Bolton, *God Has Never Failed Me, but He Sure Has Scared Me to Death a Few Times* (Tulsa: Honor Books, 1998), 80–81.

14. Andrew Carnegie, quoted in Sanborn, *The Fred Factor*, 50.

15. Ken Blanchard and Truett Cathy, *The Generosity Factor* (Grand Rapids: Zondervan, 2002), front cover jacket.

Chapter 12—A Closer Look at L.E.A.D. Them

1. Hal Reed, www.poemofquotes.com/religioustexts/bible/christian-leadership-quotes.php.
2. John C. Maxwell, *The 21 Irrefutable Laws of Leadership* (Nashville: Thomas Nelson, 1998), 203.
3. Ibid., 210.
4. Ibid., 206.
5. Smith, *Donors Are People Too*, 42.
6. Sturtevant, *The Artful Journey*, 47.

Chapter 13—A Closer Look at L.I.N.K. Them

1. Vincent Hungate, e-mail message to author, August 2006.

Chapter 14—A Closer Look at L.I.F.T. Them

1. Ralph Nichols, www.listen.org/quotations/quotes.html.
2. Callahan, *Effective Church Finances*, 141.

Chapter 15—Keys to Maintaining Strong Relationships

1. Gary Ryan Blair, en.thinkexist.com/quotes/with/keyword/results/4.html.
2. Jeavons and Basinger, *Growing Givers' Hearts*, 53.
3. Joe Tye, www.myfavoriteezines.com/ezinedirectory/quotes-about-making-difference.html.
4. Eliza Cook, www.gigausa.com/quotes/authors/eliza_cook_a001.htm.
5. Lloyd Perry, *Getting the Church on Target* (Chicago: Moody Press, 1977), 46.
6. Author unknown, "Ten Commandments of Human Relations," www.letswrap.com/LetsWRAP/Summer97/command.htm.

Chapter 16—Life Is About Relationships

1. "Relationships: The New Bottom Line in Business," *Fast Company*,
   January 1, 1995, www.fastcompany.com/events/realtime/
   florida/rlewin.html.
2. Callahan, *Effective Church Finances*, 118.